What p€
Taking O₁

MW01030261

"Decide *now* to have a better life—free of constant emotional stress, miscommunication, pent-up anger, and out-of-control responses. In *Taking Out Your Emotional Trash,* Georgia Shaffer provides mentally healthy choices and a workable plan of action. Whether you have your own emotional clutter or live with people who are stuck in the rut of unforgiveness and unfulfilled expectations, this book is the tool you need to move into emotional and spiritual health."

Carol Kent, speaker and author,
A New Kind of Normal; Between a Rock and a Grace Place

"As our level of emotional stress rises, so does the need for Georgia Shaffer's *Taking Out Your Emotional Trash.* Whether we hoard our feelings or unload them on those closest to us, we can all benefit from this excellent resource. If you are a parent, counselor, pastor, life coach, or simply want to strengthen your closest relationships, I highly recommend this book."

Dwight Bain, Executive Director of Christian Coaching Alliance,
nationally certified counselor, certified life coach

"At first glance, you might be tempted to think that you don't have enough 'emotional trash' to worry about. However, you may be surprised to discover what God has planned for you by reading this insightful book. Georgia skillfully yet gently leads you through the process necessary to clear heart and mind of emotions that may be keeping you from experiencing the abundant life Jesus came to give. I'm really glad I read it!"

Candy Davison, Women's Ministry Coordinator,
Sandy Cove Ministries

"Broken lives, broken dreams, broken hearts. All this brokenness means the emotional trash is piling high in most of our lives. I am thankful Georgia Shaffer has written a book that is better than a dumpster, trash compactor, and garbage bag in getting the junk out of our hearts, minds, and lives so we can have the life and the love we dream of, the life God intended for us, the life that brings 'a future and a hope.'"

Pam Farrel, author,
Men Are like Waffles, Women Are like Spaghetti;
Love, Honor and Forgive

"Our emotional well-being is vitally connected to our spiritual health and maturity. Georgia Shaffer guides us on a journey of transformation in *Taking Out Your Emotional Trash*. She offers practical resources so we can clear out the junk to make space for more joy, peace, and healthy relationships."

Dr. Catherine Hart Weber, therapist, teacher, author,
Flourish: Discover the Daily Joy of Abundant, Vibrant Living

"This is a much needed, practical, honest, and authentic book for those who want to develop the skills that will enable them to properly express their emotions. Georgia's own life experiences and her willingness to share it is refreshing and healing."

Michelle Cavinder, Lead Pastor,
Relational Ministries, Crystal Cathedral

Taking Out Your **Emotional** Trash

Georgia Shaffer

HARVEST HOUSE PUBLISHERS

EUGENE, OREGON

Cover photo © PhotoAlto / SuperStock

Cover by Left Coast Design, Portland, Oregon

Published in association with the Books & Such Literary Agency, 52 Mission Circle, Suite 122, PMB 170, Santa Rosa, CA 95409-5370, www.booksandsuch.biz.

Some names, histories, and details have been changed to protect the privacy of the people who shared their stories.

TAKING OUT YOUR EMOTIONAL TRASH
Copyright © 2010 by Georgia Shaffer
Published by Harvest House Publishers
Eugene, Oregon 97402
www.harvesthousepublishers.com

Library of Congress Cataloging-in-Publication Data
    Shaffer, Georgia.
    Taking out your emotional trash / Georgia Shaffer.
        p. cm.
    ISBN 978-0-7369-2726-0 (pbk.)
    1. Christian women—Religious life. 2. Emotions—Religious aspects—Christianity. I. Title.
    BV4527.S39 2010
    248.8'43—dc22
                                                                    2010009383

Printed in the United States of America

11 12 13 14 15 16 17 18 / BP-SK / 10 9 8 7 6 5 4

*To those who wish to get rid of the emotional trash
that hinders so you can experience more
peace, joy, and love in your lives and relationships.
By picking up this book you've shown you have
the heart, honesty, and courage needed to succeed.*

Acknowledgments

I am deeply grateful to my early-in-the-writing-process readers (friends and colleagues) who sacrificed their valuable time to help refine my writing: *Leslie Vernick*, *Laura Stufflebam*, and the *Lancaster writers' group*.

Special thanks to *Linda Jewell*, my "trash talking" friend. You encouraged me to visit a recycling center and landfill, clipped articles on trash, prayed with me, and spent many hours helping me verbalize my thoughts.

My deepest gratitude goes to *Deb Haggerty* who read and reread this manuscript at least three times. Your friendship is such a gift.

Thanks are also due to *Deb Strubel* for her early editorial suggestions and support. They were invaluable in helping me keep on keeping on.

To my editorial team at Harvest House: *Terry Glaspey*, *Hope Lyda*, and *Barbara Gordon*. Please know how much you are appreciated. It's a joy to work with you.

I want to thank *Mom*, *Aunt Cecelia*, *Penny Olivieri*, *Sue Smith*, and *Marilyn Neuber Larson*. You encouraged and supported me in numerous ways, especially in your prayers.

To *Rex*; my son, *Kyle*; my daughter-in-law, *Jillian*. Each of you are a special blessing in my life.

Contents

Are You Trash Conscious?

I love walking on the beach on warm summer days. But on this July morning, no matter how intently I tried to focus on the natural beauty around me, all the trash on the beach and in the water ruined my serenity. A tattered piece of rope, a white plastic tub with two decaying fish inside, a used bandage, flip-flops in various sizes and colors, broken sunglasses, a dirty T-shirt, and crushed soda cans assaulted my senses.

I wasn't the only one distracted by the debris that had washed ashore. My five-year-old nephew, Mackinley, proudly held up one large sneaker. "Hey, look what I found," he proclaimed.

"Looks like it will take you a few years to grow into that. Did you find the other one?" I asked.

"Noooo," he said as he dropped it and bent down to tug at a thick rusty wire partially buried in the sand.

"Mackinley!" my brother called as he ran to catch up with us. "I'll get that!" He carefully uncovered Mackinley's newfound treasure.

"That's really dangerous!" I said as I shook my head in disgust. "It's good we found that before someone stepped on it."

Later that day I noticed a few people on the beach picking up the litter around them, but most people simply ignored it. Since it was a public beach and municipal workers periodically removed the debris, perhaps those who came to relax felt it wasn't their responsibility. The vacationers swam, built sand castles, and relaxed along the water's edge, giving little attention to the garbage. They'd grown used to it, I guess. But on this day my consciousness about the danger and unpleasantness of trash was raised to a higher level of concern.

A Different, More Devastating Type of Garbage

There is another kind of rubbish we tend to ignore and grow used to. This kind of garbage slowly accumulates and pollutes our hearts. Let's call it "emotional trash." What does it consist of? Unrealistic expectations, frustrations, and irritations that turn into long-held resentments, deep hurts, bitterness, envy, arrogance, unforgiveness, rage, and even shame. Like the rusty wire my nephew found, these attitudes and feelings lie partially hidden in our hearts. They can hinder our growth in many areas. They're dangerous to our well-being and can negatively impact the people around us.

Unlike the public beach, however, no paid employee will periodically come and remove our junk. That task is ours and ours alone. How we do this is what this book is about. Although it will entail some work, I assure you the effort is worth it. When we notice and deal with our emotional trash, we'll encounter a remarkable peace we never dreamed possible. We'll be less stressed, better able to appreciate the beauty around us, and happier in our day-to-day lives.

Admittedly, most of us don't enjoy dealing with our trash. But if we will do the sometimes painful work of identifying and processing our junk, we'll soon discover that God, the Master of Waste Management,[1] can transform our seemingly worthless rubble into something of value. But just like the garbage collectors who only take what we drag to the curb, God won't take our trash from us unless we give it to him. Until we do that, we won't get to experience fully how he can replace our hurts, pain, and shame with his peace and joy.

The first step in removing the trash, like dealing with any other problem, is to be aware of it, to admit its existence. Just because we hide it, deny it's there, or have learned to live with it doesn't mean the garbage has disappeared or doesn't have a significant impact. In fact, it continues to pile up. Like an overflowing trash can, our neglected emotional garbage becomes a very real, smelly eyesore.

Through this book I'll help you identify some of your trash, offer guidelines for deciding what can be reused, what can be recycled, what can be tossed, and what can be done to reduce trash-producing situations. As we explore healthy ways to handle difficult and negative emotions, I'll show you methods to sort through them, give you constructive ways to handle them, and reveal options to keep negative emotional situations from becoming overwhelming or getting out of control.

This is an interactive book that you can use on your own or in a small-group setting with people you trust and respect. I encourage you to make notes in the margins as thoughts and feelings come to you. This will help you deal with them and give you references for discussion if you choose to share your insights with others.

To help you better understand where you are now and how to move forward, each chapter concludes with "Taking Out the Trash" questions. I've included room for writing, but you may want to get a notebook or journal so you have the space to go into more detail. Journaling is a great way to track your progress, sort out your thoughts, and realize more fully what's going on with you.

Maintaining Your Healthy Heart

Several years after that unpleasant day at the beach, I walked along a different shoreline. It was another gorgeous summer day. Four dolphins leaped gracefully in the waves, a group of sandpipers darted back and forth on shore, and a monarch butterfly glided in front of me. In contrast to the former trashy beach, this one was pristine. I found it much easier to experience the exquisite beauty and peace of God's creation because I wasn't distracted by garbage lying around.

Later, when I walked back to the beach entrance, I noticed one reason this area was trash free. Hanging on a post was a dispenser of plastic bags printed with the slogan "Leave no trace…take your waste!" The park service had recognized that with people there would be trash, and they wisely provided a way for garbage disposal. And most of the visitors were willingly cooperating. The result was impressive.

Just like providing ways to handle trash on the beach, if we want intimate relationships, solid careers, healthy bodies, and powerful minds, we need to clean up the old trash and create routines that will assist us in recognizing the debris in our hearts. These habits will help us handle emotions as we experience them and keep negative ones from accumulating.

I'm delighted that you refuse to stay stuck with the junk and you're ready to transform your heart into a place of joy and peace. You won't regret it!

1

Are You in the Danger Zone?

While discussing this book, a friend suggested I visit a landfill to observe how garbage is handled. That sounded like a good way to pick up some ideas so I followed her advice. As I approached the main gate of the facility, I noticed high netting surrounding the multi-acre landfill. The netting was firmly secured to huge 40-foot poles. In one section the poles were broken and the netting lay sprawled across the ground.

"What happened there?" I asked the landfill manager as I pointed to the problem area.

He replied, "The other day strong winds swept up the lighter paper garbage as it was being unloaded from the trucks. Before we could stop it, the winds plastered the paper trash against the netting. It created such a force that it broke those poles in two."

He didn't look too happy as he continued. "The accumulation of that paper created the effect of wind pushing against the sail of a boat. Instead of the wind blowing *through* the netting, it blew against the wall of debris and snapped those wooden poles like they were toothpicks." He shook his head. "It made quite a mess. Paper trash was everywhere."

As I looked at the fallen poles I thought, *What a great image of the damage that results from the accumulation of negative thoughts and feelings in us. A simple or single emotional reaction may seem as harmless as a single sheet of paper floating around a landfill. But when we allow our annoyances, anger, and frustrations to collect, these feelings become a force so powerful it can cause severe damage.*

I knew what that felt like. Recently my self-control snapped much like those fallen poles. Maybe you've had one of these weeks too. First, the red light on my printer kept flashing. No matter how many times I unplugged, replugged, and rebooted the printer and computer, the light kept flashing. On…off…on…off. I tried to ignore it, but my irritation kept building.

Next, my broadband telephone service failed. No dial tone. No incoming calls. After many hours and eight cell phone calls to customer service, I exploded when one of the techies announced, "I'm sure this is a very simple matter."

"Simple!" I blurted. "I have four college degrees, and one of them is in computer science. This problem is *not* simple or it would have been corrected hours ago." I threatened to drop my service and hung up. But my trials weren't over.

═══ TRASH TALK ═══

Many people are like garbage trucks. They run around full of garbage, full of frustrations, full of anger, and full of disappointment. As their garbage piles up, they need a place to dump it, and sometimes they'll dump it on you.

HANK MERGES

The following morning I headed to an electronics store to have a CD player installed in my car. I'd been told on the phone a few days earlier that they didn't take appointments, but if I arrived before eight o'clock I would have the shortest waiting time. I made sure I got there early. Twenty minutes after eight I discovered the installation service person hadn't yet arrived. An hour later he still hadn't shown up.

I strode up to the counter and said, "You mean I got up early on a Saturday morning just to stand around and wait for an installer to arrive?" I knew my anger wasn't going to change things, but I kept fuming while I waited. It was eleven-thirty before a tech person arrived. With an indignant huff, I marched off to the bookstore next door, bought a cup of tea, sat down in a comfy chair, and took a deep breath. Forced to sit still, I pondered my mini-meltdowns over the last few days. In addition to the printer, phone, and installation hassles, there also had been glitches in some human connections. I recalled my conversation with a good friend the day before. Although we usually chat for at least an hour, after I dumped all my woes on her, she quickly said, "I'm sorry but I need to run."

And then there was the time when my son and I exchanged ugly words. My mother and I also had a bit of a misunderstanding, and I was still seething about an issue at church. As I took in the big picture, it hit me. Each of those seemingly insignificant feelings were like individual pieces of trash paper. When blown around by frustrating circumstances, they had accumulated to the point that they pushed against the limits of my control and finally broke through. As a result, I was spreading emotional and relational litter all over those around me. I realized that if I wanted to avoid reaching that breaking point and expressing my emotions destructively, I needed to be intentional about preventing the pileup.

Years ago I attended a seminar led by Psychologist W. Robert Nay on the topic of anger management. Many of the clients in his private practice were referred to him by the judicial system because their anger had gotten out of control. Dr. Nay said that when he speaks to these offenders about their feelings and what they noticed was going on *before* they "lost it," they often said, "I was fine until that guy cut me off in traffic. I lost it *[they snapped their fingers]* just like that."

Dr. Nay discovered that no one loses it "just like that." He says that what we fail to understand is that our level of stress, if unchecked, continues rising. The emotional pressure keeps building.[1] The cumulative force becomes so strong that when we experience one additional thing, even if it's something small such as our children refusing to follow directions or a fast-food worker getting our order wrong, we snap. We've let our emotions pile up to a dangerous level. And we augment our feelings by bringing in a sense of entitlement. For instance, if we believe life is supposed to be stress-free, that we deserve a stress-free life, and people don't meet our expectations, defy us, or displease us, we get enraged.

But we can handle emotions in a productive and healthy manner. It's the *awareness* of where we are emotionally right now and a *commitment* to change that can begin to release the pressure.

Where Are You Emotionally?

Even if you don't see yourself as an emotional person, the fact is that "emotions are a gift of God, who created each of us with a capacity to feel and express our emotions."[2] It's not that your emotions are unhealthy or dangerous. It's what you do or don't do with them that can be the problem. Your feelings have the potential to become especially harmful when you stuff them, deny them, or allow them to accumulate. When that happens, you may become controlled by them.

The following graph was adapted from an example shown at the seminar given by Dr. Nay. Zero represents no emotional pressure, no buildup of irritations, resentments, insecurities, bitterness, or negative emotions (a place where we never are). For this example, let's assume 30 is an acceptable level of stress and 80 is the point where we snap because feelings have piled up and we've failed to deal with them constructively. Like the snapped telephone poles at the landfill, we each have a point where we can't handle one more piece of trash. That is when we lose control. We cross a line, so to speak, and move into the danger zone of being controlled by our emotions. We *react* rather than *respond* to life. Because emotions have piled up and up and up, we say or do things that are unhealthy for us, hurtful for others, and harmful to our relationships.

Let's hypothetically say the pressure of your negative feelings has built up to a level of 79. You are irritated, your jaw is clenched, and your head is throbbing. But you are handling the circumstances around you without losing control. Your daughter says, "No duh, Mom," when you make a comment, and you take it in without saying or doing anything hurtful. But now you're at 79.9. One more comment, one more roll of her eyes moves you into reaction mode. You make negative comments, you stomp off, and you explode. Your daughter's action didn't cause you to snap. Since you were already at a heightened emotional level, her action put you over the edge.

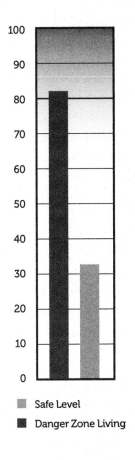

Safe Level
Danger Zone Living

If we want to maintain control and stay healthy in our emotions, we need to first understand that we don't go from a 30 to a 79 "just like that." According to Dr. Nay, people often assume they start the morning at an emotional level of 0, when in fact they may have awakened at an emotional level of 79. If we don't realize we are already at the I-can't-handle-one-more-thing-without-losing-it point, we won't do anything to relieve the emotional pressure. So when "one more thing" happens, we'll probably do or say something we regret and make our situation worse.

Emotional awareness is realizing "there is an emotional impact from almost every stimulus received and every response you give. You may not feel them all consciously, but all of these tiny subconscious emotional stimuli are adding pressure and intensity to the way you respond all throughout the day."[3] This accumulation of emotional pressure from annoyances, frustrations, and feelings of entitlement are like the papers that piled against the netting at the landfill. The force of the wind plastered the papers against the net and then snapped the poles. In the same way, it usually isn't just one emotion that puts us in an emotional danger zone. Instead it's the sadness + frustration + embarrassment + disappointment + jealousy + anger that we ignore or stuff or allow to accumulate. The cumulative effect can be disastrous.

Looking back at the graph, the shorter bar could represent my emotional buildup at the beginning of that difficult week. The taller bar could symbolize that Saturday morning when I raised my voice at the person behind the electronics counter just before I turned around with a huff and stomped out the door.

For many of us, the daily minor irritations, frustrations, and emotional upsets can accumulate and sneak up on us. We may realize the emotional ramifications of something major, such as a death in the family and the overwhelming sadness and anger that brings. But the tiny upsets sidle by us unnoticed until suddenly, "just like that," we're at the breaking point. And then we pay the price relationally. The cost may be something as simple as everyone thinking we have a lousy attitude and would we please go somewhere else or as permanent as a ruptured relationship.

TRASH TALK

Practice the art of identifying emotional garbage.

RANDY SCHUTT

Kayla ignored her emotions for weeks. Then one day she was late for work because she overslept and couldn't find her keys. Next she got stuck in traffic and realized she'd forgotten her lunch. By the time Kayla got to work, she'd crossed into the danger zone without realizing it. She snapped at the office manager and treated her boss disrespectfully because she hadn't paid attention to the state of her emotions and dealt with the overload.

Garrison, on the other hand, told me he stuffs minor annoyances. "Right now I'm dating someone. She might make a comment unintentionally that hurts me. Instead of saying anything, I think, *It's not that big of a deal so why create conflict?* But after weeks and weeks of stuffing these little hurts and annoyances, I blow up and say all kinds of nasty things to her. This type of behavior ended my last relationship."

We don't all react like Kayla, who became snappish, or Garrison, who became verbally aggressive, when we're living in the danger zone. Meltdown moments and reactions will be different from person to person. Some of us tend to be forceful verbally or even physically. Others become sarcastic, making cutting comments that hurt others deeply. Some withdraw, become numb, or cry. Perhaps you've recently lost your cool and made a snide remark to that tech person who spoke limited English. Maybe you snapped at that clerk you thought incompetent. Or perhaps you found yourself saying things as a parent you vowed you'd never say, such as, "Won't you ever get it right? How stupid can you get?"

For most of us who cross the line and find ourselves reacting badly, our behaviors are hard to recognize because they're so subtle. Maybe when you are ticked off with your spouse, you walk away and for the next couple of days give him or her the silent treatment. You isolate yourself and refuse to discuss the problem at hand. Or maybe you're the kind of person who remains polite, but you withhold the very thing you know someone wants, such as quality time, affection, or appreciation.

Recognizing when we aren't handling things well and how we react negatively are key factors in managing our emotions.

Commitment to Change

I mentioned earlier that it's the *awareness of where we are emotionally* and *the commitment to change* that enables us to reverse our tendency to react rather than respond to our emotions. Perhaps you're reading this book because your relationships are falling apart. Or maybe you're unhappy with your life and are desperate to change it, but you don't know where to start. Do you know you'll be much more likely to make and keep a commitment to handle your feelings differently if you are emotionally invested in the process? Make a change decision from your heart. You can explore where you are by asking:

- What will motivate me to pay attention to how my behavior affects others?

- What will inspire me to get serious about dealing with my emotional stuff?

The best way to succeed in altering behavior is to find some meaningful, lasting reasons for implementing the changes. Here are some reasons you may identify with. After reading through them, why not checkmark the ones that you can relate to? After you read these, feel free to add more reasons that apply to your situation in the margins so you can refer back to them when you need encouragement.

- You want to be a good role model for your children and grandchildren. Maybe you've noticed lately how your children are displaying the same out-of-control behaviors you are. Instead of feeling guilty, choose to learn the skills needed to minimize the time you live in the danger zone.

- Growing emotionally and spiritually is extremely important to you. You aren't having serious relationship problems, but you are feeling stuck. You want to do something differently, but you're not sure what to do or how to do it.

- Your closest relationships are deteriorating because of your insecurities, jealousies, and anxiety. Your spouse has given you an ultimatum, "You need to do something about this or else."

- You've become aware that your anger, frustrations, and resentment are affecting your performance at work. Your supervisor has suggested you get help. You want to control your emotions instead of allowing them to control you.

- Your friends are distancing themselves. Instead of having fun with them you've been bogged down trying to clean up the emotional messes you've created in your relationships.

- You've procrastinated in dealing with some of your emotional reactions because you figured everything would work out on its own. You now realize that's not going to happen. You don't want to pretend any longer. You know that life will be easier if you deal with your problems now.

- You yearn for deep, meaningful relationships but your constant moodiness has fractured friendships at church, work, and socially.

- You're eating or drinking too much because you don't know how to deal with the stuff in your heart and life.

- You always thought your junk was your junk and nobody else needed to know about it until a close friend helped you realize your "private" stuff was impacting people around you. You want to cultivate desirable qualities that attract people.

- Your poor physical health is motivating you to get serious about improving your emotional health. Your habit of not talking about feelings has created all sorts of health-related problems, such as insomnia, high blood pressure, and headaches. You want to change so you're not as easily fatigued, you can think more clearly, and you're healthier overall.

Even when we are inspired to change, change is hard. In the short-term, it seems much easier and more comfortable to just stay the same. But avoiding change creates more pain in the long term. So whether your motivation is to have better health, richer relationships, or to stop contaminating your current ones, take a moment to clarify, write down, and tell at least one person why you are going to change the way you've been handling your emotions.

- I'm tired of reacting negatively because…

- When I change reacting to responding, I should notice…

- This week I'm going to tell [*person's name*] about my plans to change how I handle my emotions.

Routine Trips to the Dumpster

Did you know that even on the most basic, cellular level of our bodies there is an intricate system for managing waste? According to medical research, our "cells have developed complex systems for recycling, reusing, and disposing of damaged, nonfunctional waste proteins." Inside of us we have little "garbage collectors." When working properly, they remove the trash from each cell and prevent disease. If these collectors fail to operate correctly, proteins can accumulate in the cell, become toxic, and cause disease.[4]

Now that you've made the commitment to become healthier when it comes to your emotions, your first step is to establish the habit of routinely taking your emotional trash to the dumpster. Just as our healthy cells process waste regularly, we want to routinely deal with our emotions to keep us in a safe zone. We need to monitor ourselves, recognize when our emotions are piling up, and take action to prevent hazardous situations.

One way to "check in" with ourselves is to set aside time to reflect and pray on what we're saying and doing. Until that Saturday morning in the bookstore after my meltdown at the electronics store, I hadn't been paying attention to how my trash was accumulating. I hadn't noticed because for weeks I'd been caught up in the busyness of meeting various deadlines. I'd let my normal routines slide and omitted time for spiritual self-examination, prayer, journaling, and addressing my emotions. The result was extra stress and not being gracious to the people around me.

Perhaps if I hadn't been so driven to complete my to-do list I would have noticed the signals that would have alerted me that I was fast approaching overload. I was feeling dissatisfied with everyone and everything. I was focused solely on *my* problems and not considering the concerns of others. I'd neglected my basic needs, such as eating healthy foods and getting enough rest. The muscles in my shoulders were hard and tight, and I'd been experiencing headaches.

We all have times when we break our routines to deal with the urgent. And that's okay. But unless we're also attentive to how our emotions are building to critical mass, we'll find ourselves in trouble before we know it. But if we make the adjustments necessary to deal with our grudges, hurts, and irritations as we go along, we'll cut down on how often our negative emotions control us.

The list on the next page will help you know what to look for and be sensitive to so you will know if you're approaching the danger zone. Use it as you would a mirror or scale to check out how you're doing. And if you can identify other behaviors that may indicate

I AM...

- feeling like I'm always on edge.

- becoming driven and anxious.

- suffering from tight muscles and tension headaches.

- looking to others to make me happy.

- needing a break but can't take time off work.

- losing sight of the big picture.

- becoming too protective of my time and energy.

- blowing issues out of proportion.

- beating myself up by thinking *How stupid can I be?* and *Can't I do anything right?*

- neglecting basic needs, such as eating well and sleeping enough.

- not thinking about the needs of others.

- becoming easily hurt and offended.

- focusing solely on my problems and my world.

- feeling dissatisfied with everything and everyone.

- hungering for approval and affirmation.

-

-

-

you're about to be carried away by your emotions, add them to the list. Feel free to make a copy of this list and post it where you'll see it so you can regularly check on your progress.

While everyone has bad days, you'll want to pay attention to anything that is becoming a *pattern* in your life. The goal is to stop the accumulation of emotional trash *before* the bin overflows and *reduce* the amount of emotional garbage generated. When you set aside time for maintenance and remember to take the emotional junk to the dumpster, you'll experience less stress, a healthier body, stronger relationships, and better attitudes.

TAKING OUT THE TRASH

1. Trash that we allow to pile up creates harmful conditions. Dealing with or emptying emotional trash reduces our stress and creates healthier conditions emotionally, physically, and mentally. Do you tend to allow your emotions to pile up? Do you know why?

   • Do you usually *react* to situations or *respond* to them? Explain.

   • What does that tell you about how you handle your emotions? Do you need to make some changes? What is the next step God is showing you?

2. Describe how emotions were handled in your home when you were growing up.

   • Did your parents discuss their feelings? Did your parents discuss and accept your feelings?

- Did your family wait for a crisis before they dealt with feelings?

- Did you grow up thinking you were the only person who ever felt angry or sad or frustrated?

3. What do your meltdown moments usually look like?

   ☐ Do you get snappy with others?

   ☐ Do you withdraw and give the silent treatment?

   ☐ Do you yell or curse?

   ☐ Do you remain polite but watch for an opportunity to get even?

   ☐ Do you punch things or hit people or animals?

   ☐ Other (describe):

   ☐ Other (describe):

4. How often would those closest to you say you live in the danger zone? How often would they say you get really close to or in the danger zone?

   - Do people say they have to treat you with kid gloves or feel like they're walking on eggshells around you?

- How often do you say or do something you later regret?

- How frequently do you *fail* to say or do something and regret it later?

2

What Trash Have You Grown Used To?

My aunts and I spent weeks sorting through my grandfather's possessions. We separated out the important items and divided what remained into piles of stuff that needed to be trashed, recycled, or taken to a local charity. Before the truck arrived to haul away the stuff, we decided to recheck to make sure there was nothing of sentimental value in the "get rid of" stacks.

That morning I kept looking at the area rug on my grandfather's hardwood living room floor. No one had expressed any interest in the 9 x 12 rug, and I wondered why I was even considering it. Grandpa purchased it at an auction later in life, so I didn't have any childhood memories associated with it. I found the rug's dull-gray background and maroon designs unattractive. *But maybe Kyle could use it when he heads to college in a couple of years,* I thought. On a whim I asked my aunts, "What do you think this rug is worth?" (We had decided to pay Grandpa's estate the estimated value of any item we chose to keep so heirs would get fair shares.)

"It's yours for $25," one of my aunts said.

I paid for it and hauled it home.

That rug remained rolled up in the garage for almost two years. Several times I considered putting it out with the trash, but I didn't.

Finally I decided to have a professional cleaner freshen it up. A few days later this "strictly about business" cleaner called me with an excitement in his voice I'd never heard before. "Georgia, you won't believe it! You have to see this Oriental rug. It's beautiful!" He caught his breath. "It looks nothing like the rug I picked up. I wished I'd taken a before picture. And the rug isn't gray—it's beige."

"You're kidding!" I responded. "It's an Oriental rug?"

"Yes. It has intricate designs and a border around the edge. It's gorgeous compared to what it looked like. I can't wait for you to see it. By the way, when I researched the rug I found that it dates back to the 1920s."

Sure enough, when it was delivered a few days later I couldn't believe the transformation. All that beauty had been hidden under layers of ground-in dirt. Needless to say, that rug never did end up in my son's college apartment.

I've often wondered how that rug became so deeply embedded with dirt. I assume it happened slowly, over a lot of time, and it was never given a deep cleaning. Everyone grew so used to the soiled look that no one remembered the beauty of its original design.

Sadly, just like my grandfather's rug, our hearts can become slowly embedded with "dirt"—prideful thoughts, unforgiveness, and feelings of entitlement ("I deserve...")—and we don't even notice how much beauty we've lost in our lives.

Kristin experienced this truth when she cared for her elderly mother who had been in a car accident. Kristin snapped at her mother over the most insignificant things. Every little request her mother made, even things like "Will you buy me some hand cream?" felt like a huge assignment. After praying about her short fuse, Kristin realized her rotten attitude had more to do with what was in her heart than what her mother expected or required. So Kristin asked God to show her what *he* wanted her to see about her behavior. A few weeks later he revealed the root of her troubling mindset.

Through a casual conversation with an old friend from high school, Kristin realized her poor attitude grew from something she'd held on to for years. While growing up, she and her three sisters had to care for themselves because their mother was frequently absent with work, church, and social activities. Decades later, by reversing roles and taking on responsibilities as her mother's caregiver, Kristin realized she was bitter about the lack of maternal attention and care during her at-home years. Especially surprising to Kristin, who was now in her fifties, was that she'd harbored this load of resentment without any conscious awareness of it for more than 40 years.

As a psychologist I hear stories like this all the time. Like Kristin's bitterness, there are many attitudes, thoughts, and feelings in our hearts that we fail to see even though they negatively influence our lives and relationships. As Jesus said, "From within, out of a person's heart, come evil thoughts, sexual immorality, theft, murder, adultery, greed, wickedness, deceit, lustful desires, envy, slander, pride, and foolishness" (Mark 7:21-22 NLT).

You may be wondering, *Why can't I clearly see things, such as pride, that lie deep within my heart? I'm not deliberately trying to hide or ignore problems.* While there are many reasons for limited insights, sometimes we are blind to the truth because, like the dirt ground into my grandfather's rug, we've simply grown used to things as they are.

Have you noticed how some people who live near a fast-food restaurant get used to the smell of grilled meat or spices? Or how people who are sloppy can't see the extent of their sloppiness but everyone else can? In the same way, we get used to the darkness in our hearts. We don't see the dirt. We don't even realize that a deep cleaning is needed.

What You've Been Missing

God is able to shed his light in the darkest areas of your heart to reveal what you need to see. Like the professional rug cleaner who uncovered the beautiful design in my grandfather's rug, God can be your Master Cleaner. You only need to ask him to help and then be still, expectant, quietly listening, and ready to follow his counsel.

Asking for God's Help

We all have plenty of heart junk, and only God knows everything that is in us and how best to remove it. When I was researching how Oriental rugs are to be cleaned, I was fascinated to learn that one rug cleaning service used patented tools that gently expelled *several pounds* of dust and debris that regular vacuuming couldn't remove. Isn't that amazing?

One of the tools we can use for deep cleaning our hearts is God's Word. And we even have help available for understanding it! Jesus said, "When he, the Spirit of truth, comes, he will guide you into all truth. He will not speak on his own; he will speak only what he hears, and he will tell you what is yet to come" (John 16:13). One of my favorite verses to pray when asking God to show me what is lodged deep in my heart is Psalm 139:23:

> Search me, O God, and know my heart;
>> test me and know my anxious thoughts.
> See if there is any offensive way in me,
>> and lead me in the way everlasting.

Sometimes God will show me a hurt I've failed to forgive. One morning during my quiet time with him, I was reading Isaiah 43. Two verses jumped off the page: "Forget the former things; do not dwell on the past" (Isaiah 43:18) and "I, even I, am he who blots out your transgressions, for my own sake, and remembers your sins no more" (Isaiah 43:25).

The night before I'd shared with a friend how someone we both knew had deeply hurt me with his actions two years earlier. I shared every little detail of what he'd done. After reading those Scriptures the following morning, I became aware of what I was doing. I was tightly holding on to grudges and reliving them by repeating to all who would listen what had been done to me. God reminded me that when I mess up he forgives me without telling anyone else about my sins or repeating my wrongs over and over again.

I knew I needed to admit my unforgiveness and ask God to heal and restore my heart. That simple prayer made a dramatic difference. I couldn't believe how light and free I felt compared to the months before. I wondered, *Georgia, why did you hold on to those grudges for so long?* But I knew why. I'd grown used to them. They'd become such a part of me that I didn't notice how unattractive they were. It wasn't until I prayed to God and read those Scripture verses that I was able to stop concentrating on what someone had done to me and allow God to show me what I was continuing to do.

Other times, when I've asked God for help, he's used Scripture to show me a wrong motive I didn't see. Verses from the Bible have also revealed my critical spirit and pride to help me understand how I'd made a project, person, or thing more important than God.

TRASH TALK

It is so hard to look deep inside yourself. My experience has been that very few people do the long, hard work of the soul. Maybe that's why Jesus said the way is narrow.

ROB BELL

The willingness to ask God to help us look deeply into our souls is not for the purpose of focusing on all the things that are wrong or horrible with us. It's not about getting totally absorbed in ourselves and ignoring others. Rather, the goal is to acknowledge our dirt—our faults—and allow God to vacuum out those attitudes and feelings that have soiled our inner beauty.

Be Still and Listen

For thousands of years, rug makers found that when they immersed their rugs in rivers or streams of fresh water, the water would gently lift out embedded dirt. In an effort to duplicate this process, one Oriental rug cleaning company first vacuums a rug and then immerses it in "slow moving fresh water" that has mild cleaning solutions added to it.

In the same way, "the image of refreshing water is used throughout the Bible to describe the spiritual cleansing and renewal that Jesus offers" to those of us who willingly open our hearts to him.[1] When we quietly immerse ourselves in his presence, Jesus will use his living water to gently remove layers of grime, such as arrogance or deceptive dealings, from our hearts. Unlike Satan, who tries to destroy us with his harsh spirit of condemnation and lies about our value, God lovingly cleanses us of our offensive ways. I admit there are times when God has given me a "not so gentle" cleaning, but even then I knew he was being loving. He wasn't content to leave me in such a bad state. God never makes us feel like we're hopeless, worthless human beings.

Until we know God and are still before him, listening for his wisdom, we won't be in a position to notice what he wants us to pay attention to. When we carve out time for moments of silence and solitude in the midst of the noisiness of life, we realize the truth—that "solitude will do its good work whether we know what we are doing or not."[2]

In those quiet moments, God can speak to us in many different ways—through Scripture, our circumstances, people, and even birds. One of my friends wrote this in her journal during a quiet time:

> The cries of the crows startle me from my reflective thoughts. I watch as the birds descend upon the tree and into the deep branches. The green foliage is so dense that they disappear from my sight.
>
> I wonder how I remain hidden and blind to myself in areas that should be seen. Do I keep a wall of protectiveness around me filled with reasons, blame, and judgment that prevents me from seeing clearly? Do I remain hidden in denial from things I need to look at?
>
> What deep, dark secrets lurk beneath my subconscious, waiting to be exposed? Is it better to say, "Come out now" while I am alone with God? If I take this time to look at some of these

hidden areas, will it protect me from something surfacing in a public forum in a not-so-nice way? Sort of like the raw, startling sound of the crows? "Ah, see me!" the crow cries. With his cry I want to say hush, too loud, too brash, no music, nothing draws me. Where is the music, the soft, melodious music?

As I ponder on the crows, I realize without quiet reflective time with God I am unable to stop the abrupt crow caws in my own life—caws of words and actions that leave people startled and hurt.

Fortunately, God sees the crows and me even in our camouflaged environment and can speak to and calm our fears. Only God can open the way for us to see and be seen. Just as the wind moves the branches to expose the crows, God moves the stumbling blocks from my heart and the scales from my eyes to see my sin.

As more of my hidden areas become exposed to God's light, I begin to be free and healthy to live the life God wants for me. My crow caws are turned into the songs of bliss, replacing hurt with love and harsh words with patience and kindness.

If my friend hadn't removed herself from the distractions of life and put herself in the position to be still and listen, would God have broken through the brash sounds of the crows to reach her heart? Would he have bypassed her blockades to restore her heart by replacing hurt with *his love* and harsh words with *his patience* and *kindness*?

Just because we pause to listen to God, however, doesn't mean there won't be times when he seems to be silent. And it's during those times that we must patiently wait.

Waiting Expectantly

When the rug cleaner had excitedly telephoned to tell me how beautiful my grandfather's rug was, one of the things he said was "I can't *wait* for you to see it!" He explained that the reason I needed to wait was because the wet rug was hanging on a large rod and needed to air dry. If he exposed the rug to high levels of heat to dry it quickly, the rug could be damaged. I did wait, and I waited expectantly.

When Kristin prayed about her snappiness with her injured mother, God didn't immediately point out her long-held resentments. No, Kristin prayed and sought his wisdom for several weeks. Then one day God lovingly showed her, through a friend, what was in her heart.

Waiting expectantly for God to do his healing work can be tough and frustrating, especially when we're in pain. Sometimes we are forced to live with the ongoing tension of not knowing what he is doing. Maybe we need to wait until he has prepared our hearts and ears to hear what he has to say. Maybe we need to wait while he prepares the heart of someone else—so that person is ready to receive our apology or restitution. Whatever the reason, we need to wait patiently and expectantly.

Gabriella felt certain that the difficulties in her marriage stemmed from her husband's controlling manner. As she prayed, listened, and sought counseling, she waited for God to clearly show her what to do. One of the things he slowly revealed to her was that while her husband needed to grow, part of the problem was *her* ongoing resentment. For more than 20 years she'd resented her husband's encouragement to get an abortion before they were married. Although Gabriella had ultimately agreed and had the procedure done, she was angry that he'd pressured her to abort the baby. She realized that until she let go of her bitterness it would continue to interfere with her ability to emotionally connect with her husband.

Like Gabriella recognizing the bitterness she carried for years, I too have found that God usually reveals information a little bit at a time and in a way that isn't condemning, but definitely convicting. We probably couldn't handle it if he revealed our stuff to us all at once. When our hearts are aligned with God on the issue he's showing to us and we are willing to do our part in cleaning out the junk by obeying him fully, that's when we can be restored to the original glory he intended for us.

Obeying Fully

I mentioned earlier that I knew God wanted me to let go of some grudges I'd been holding on to for a few years. While I knew I needed to be obedient and forgive, there was an unhealthy part of me that was comforted by embracing them. That part felt like I had a right to keep holding on to my bad attitude. I know this wasn't true or helpful, but that's how I felt at the time.

When it comes to obeying God fully and keeping the commitment you made to take out your trash, please know there is a part of you that usually continues to resist. It's normal to struggle when making real changes. Recognize and accept that there will be times when you sabotage yourself. For example, you might say, "Yes, I was nasty to my husband—but he deserved it." As long as you put the blame on someone else and make excuses for your behavior, you're turning a blind eye to your own junk.

It's so easy to discount our actions and find fault in the responses of others. It's also much less painful in the short term. I'm sure you've heard people react to a sermon or lecture with comments like "I wish my daughter could have heard this" or "Boy, my boss sure needed to hear that message."

Discounting our own issues is not only irresponsible but unbiblical. Jesus asked, "Why do you look at the speck of sawdust in your brother's eye and pay no attention to the plank in your own eye?" He warns, "First take the plank out of your own eye, and then you will see clearly to remove the speck from your brother's eye" (Matthew 7:3,5).

Isn't it interesting that Jesus says a person could metaphorically have an entire plank in one's eye and not even be aware of it? That's why Jesus tells us to pay attention to *our* faults first. When *we think* we are clearly seeing the sins of another, we are probably most blind to our own.

Until I surrendered the grudges I held against that friend, I was solidifying that junk in my heart. First John 1:9 tells us, "If we confess our sins, he is faithful and just and will forgive us our sins and purify us from all unrighteousness." When we acknowledge or admit we have trash, God promises to help us clean it up. We want to accept his forgiveness and then take whatever action he guides us to take.

Willingness to obey means, first, confessing our sin to God and agreeing with him that whatever he has shown us doesn't belong in our hearts.

TRASH TALK

At least once a day, to satisfy needs for more
energy and calm, check in with your emotions.
We don't need resentments hanging around.

RICK GOODFRIEND

We tell God what we did wrong and that we are in need of his deep cleaning. As pastor and author John Ortberg writes, "Confession is not primarily something God has us do because he needs it. God is not clutching tightly to his mercy, as if we have to pry it from his fingers like a child's last cookie. We need to confess in order to heal and be changed."[3]

Next we have to do whatever God shows us needs to be done to restore a relationship or make restitution. If we have hurt another person, God might lead us to go to that person and ask for forgiveness.

Keeping short accounts with God by frequent confessions not only enables us to remove the negative things we may have held on to for far too long, but it also minimizes the conditions that can lead to deadly actions, such as theft, murder, and adultery (Mark 7:21). One of my friends who lives in New Mexico was telling me about the black widow spiders in her area that had taken up residence in the ivy and leaf debris under her Arizona Cypress trees. The cool, dark conditions under the ivy and dead leaves provided the habitat these deadly spiders love. She said, "When I remove the ivy and plant rubbish, exposing the ground to the sun, the black widows don't find my backyard as inviting."

In the same way, by being diligent and vigilant to shine God's light in our hearts on a routine basis, we can create an environment where the dark, dirty, and even dangerous things won't take up residency.

When you willingly see your trash—the obvious and the not-so-obvious—and allow God to heal you, you will begin to notice a real change in your behavior because of the change in your heart. When you have a willingness to ask for God's help, to be still and listen quietly, to wait expectantly, and to obey fully, God can remove years of accumulated dirt and reveal his original design for you.

It's been 20 years since I had my grandfather's oriental rug professionally cleaned. It's still in my home today, and I've been very diligent about keeping it clean. It may have collected some dirt over those years, but the colors and designs are still vibrant and lovely. I plan to keep it that way, especially now that I know how beautiful it really is.

TIME TO TAKE OUT THE TRASH

1. *Ask for God's help.* We shouldn't assume that all is well in our hearts. Jesus said, "Out of the heart come evil thoughts." Until we acknowledge we have junk, we are only deceiving ourselves. How do you feel about asking God to show you what you've grown used to (being frightened, disgusted, discouraged, overwhelmed, anxious, hopeless, excited)? List any concerns you have that might prevent you from talking to him about how you feel. How can you relate this statement to where you are right now: "If you want clean dishes tomorrow, you have to handle the dirty ones today"?

2. *Be still and listen quietly.* Set aside some time regularly to sit quietly with God and allow him to speak to you. Pray that you will be open to what he wants you to see and hear: "Lord, I'm listening. Please show me what doesn't belong in my heart." If you'd like, you can write out your prayer.

3. *Wait expectantly.* Our grudges and resentments tend to be some of the things we don't notice or we hide them from ourselves. Ask God to show you if there is anything you've been holding on to that you shouldn't be. Remember God promises that the Holy Spirit will guide you and show you the truth (John 16:13). What is he revealing to you?

4. *Obey fully.* More than once in my quiet time I've realized that *I* was deciding what I needed to deal with rather than allowing God to take the lead. Ask God to expose any attitudes, thoughts, or feelings that might be keeping you from obeying him and being all he designed you to be. Be especially observant if you're telling yourself, "I have a right to get back at them" or "They deserved what they got." What keeps you from wholeheartedly obeying God?

3

How Do You Sort Through Your Emotional Trash?

One of the trends in recycling is called single-stream processing or commingling. Plastics, paper, cardboard, and most other recyclable materials no longer have to be separated. All materials go out to the curb in one container and are picked up in "one stream" by a recycling truck. (In some areas, glass is put in separate boxes for curbside pickup so workers don't worry about glass shards when sorting.) When the recyclable material arrives at the center, it is dumped in one area to be sorted by people, machines, and tools.[1]

Like the trash that arrives at the recycling center, our emotions are usually mixed together rather than neatly separated into categories of disappointment, anger, happiness, contentment, or resentment. For example, people who think things out and emphasize facts are thinking oriented. They approach life from a mental standpoint and can usually readily name their emotions. However, they have often have difficulty "feeling" them. On the other hand, people who are emotionally oriented may have difficulty identifying how they're feeling because so many emotionally related thoughts are flooding their minds. These people tend to base decisions on their emotional state rather than using a more cognitive approach. Before we can effectively process our emotions, we need to understand what tools are available to help us dump out and sort through our feelings.

While most people don't have too much trouble in the physical realm with what to keep, what to discard, and what to recycle, it's a little harder sorting through the many emotions we experience. Are we feeling embarrassed or afraid? Betrayed or abandoned? Rejected or enraged?

Several years ago I co-led an educational event with a friend. We both have strong personalities and like to be in control, but because we respect each other's opinions we usually work well together. At this event, however, we clashed more than once. By the fifth day and last session, I was worn out. When my colleague made a slightly negative remark, I felt annoyed and ready to lash out.

The next morning I thought about what had happened. I struggled to sort through my emotions. I knew I felt upset, but I wasn't quite sure why it was so strong. Was there jealousy between us? Was I feeling misunderstood? Was I wallowing in self-pity, feeling hurt, or just plain angry? Was I being too sensitive to criticism and overreacting to her comments?

TRASH TALK

To instruct us in candid honesty, God gave us the
book of Psalms—a worship manual full of ranting,
raving, doubts, fears, resentments, and deep passions
combined with thanksgiving, praise, and statements
of faith. Every possible emotion is catalogued.

RICK WARREN

I've learned that instead of stewing about these kinds of situations, I can take action. First, I dump my feelings in a safe way. Then I take some time to sort through them and name what I'm feeling. Even though this may sound simplistic, it's not always easy. When I have a lot of thoughts and emotions running around in my head and heart, I use a list of "feeling words" I keep in my journal to help me choose. Glancing over the words reminds me of the many descriptions available and helps me clarify what I'm feeling. There are many such lists available on the Internet, but I've provided a sampling of words on the next page to help you get started right away.[2] Positive feelings weren't included because people usually don't struggle with identifying them.

Simply reading through a list of emotions may not be enough. There are several additional ways to identify feelings. When you're stirred up and confused, you can sort out feelings as you pray, read Scripture, journal your thoughts, talk with someone you trust, do something physical, or take time for rest and renewal. Using a combination of several things usually provides the best results.

If this process feels awkward or it's not always the first thing you think of when you're upset, that's okay. Sorting through feelings is a *learned* activity. When my son, Kyle, was little, he struggled to express himself verbally and interact appropriately with others. Early in his preschool years his teacher followed him around and helped him communicate with his peers. For example, if Kyle wanted a toy, he would typically lunge for it. But his teacher would physically hold him back and identify what he was feeling and wanting. "Kyle would like to play with that toy, but right now he is going to wait until someone is not playing with it," she'd say. As he matured, he learned the vocabulary and patience to express what he wanted to say and convey what he was feeling on his own. Pinpointing emotions and what's going on inside of us is a skill you can master.

Let's take a closer look at the various tools or techniques and how they work.

Praying for Direction and Clarity

One of the ways we show God he is first in our lives is by going to him with our problems and concerns. Whether we begin praying by sharing our complaints or thanking him for listening, it's important to seek his wisdom. Communicating with God in an honest way isn't always pretty, but we can be assured that God will not reject

FEELING WORDS

abandoned	criticized	enraged	miserable
abused	crummy	exasperated	mortified
accused	crushed	frightened	neglected
agitated	cynical	grumpy	numb
alienated	deceived	guilty	offended
annoyed	defeated	hateful	panicky
anxious	defenseless	heartbroken	pressured
ashamed	dejected	horrified	puzzled
attacked	demeaned	humiliated	regretful
avoided	deprived	inadequate	remorseful
awkward	desperate	incensed	shocked
belittled	disappointed	incompetent	suspicious
betrayed	discouraged	indifferent	tense
blamed	disgraced	insecure	threatened
brushed-off	disillusioned	insensitive	uncertain
burdened	dismayed	insignificant	unnoticed
challenged	disoriented	jealous	unwanted
condemned	displeased	lifeless	vengeful
conflicted	dissatisfied	listless	weary
controlled	distrustful	lost	worthless
crazed	edgy	manipulated	

us because he loves us. And he already knows how we're feeling, so he won't be surprised or shocked.

To identify your feelings in prayer start with the word "I." For instance, when I'm upset I tell God that although *I* understand he is in control and *I* will trust him, *I* don't like what he has allowed to happen. *I* do not like it one little bit. Starting with the word "I" helps me unravel what's going on inside of me.

Many Christians are concerned that God will be offended if they direct their complaints his way. Author and pastor John Ortberg suggests that rather than being offended, God encourages our heart-revealing sharing: "The most frequent psalm consists of somebody complaining to God." Ortberg urges us to have the courage to face our feelings instead of hiding our discouragement.[3]

We want to be brutally honest before God, but accusing him of wrongdoing is counterproductive. When I feel as if God isn't doing what *I* think needs to be done, I put it this way: "I know you are perfectly just, God, but right now I feel as if things aren't fair." Sometimes I ask, "Lord, why is this bothering me so much?" or "I can't name what I'm feeling. Will you help me figure it out?"

Praying not only helps us identify our emotions, but it also reduces our tendency to dwell on them, which keeps us from getting more and more upset. With God's help we can gain more control of our feelings so we can let go of them or transform them into something constructive. Our human tendency is to call another person when we're upset and unload as we process the negative emotions. This isn't always the wisest choice. We may feel better, but sometimes our friends and family may feel dumped on. Always ask, "Is this something I need to talk with God about first?"

Another plus to bringing our negative emotions before the Lord is that we safeguard our reputations from people we may think are worthy of our trust but turn out not to be. More than one person has experienced the betrayal and hurt that resulted from a confidence unwisely shared.

Read Scripture

Acknowledging our feelings doesn't mean ignoring the truths from Scripture. Feelings come and go. Just because we *feel* something is true doesn't mean it is true. When I was diagnosed with cancer more than 20 years ago, I felt frightened, discouraged, and confused. I called a friend, Marita, and asked her to pray for me. As we talked I said, "I don't feel God, and I want to feel him." Marita emailed my prayer request to several people, and the next day another friend sent me this in response: "Georgia, you don't need to feel God. You *know* him." Scripture says that no matter how we feel at the moment, God will *never* leave or forsake us!

As you read the Bible during your turmoil, ask God to show you his truths. Here are some questions you can ask God as you delve into his Word:

- What do you want to show me *about me* in this passage?

- What do you want to show me *about you* in this passage?

- How do you want me to respond to the situation I'm dealing with?

- What truth am I ignoring?

You may also want to ask God to lead you to the verses you need right now. Here are some passages that have helped me process and give voice to my emotions:

- Psalm 22 when I'm overwhelmed by circumstances.

- Psalm 51 when I'm aware of my failings and in desperate need of God's forgiveness.

- Psalm 102 when I'm feeling sick, rejected, or tossed aside.

- Job 38–42 when I'm confused, angry, and questioning God. (These chapters help me remember how powerful and awesome God is.)

Journal Your Thoughts and Experiences

All the distractions of daily living can leave us feeling stretched and scattered. When we take the time to write and reflect, we can better focus on what's bugging us. Sometimes we are able to see a recent issue more clearly, while at other times we may gain a fresh perspective on an old problem. Journaling also lets us write about our hurts and frustrations without being concerned we'll say something that will offend someone or reveal something we might later regret. And there's no one to mock our feelings or berate our views.

Journaling is one of the best ways I've found to work through things. My journal is a safe place to shed my irritations, unload toxic thoughts, and determine what I'm feeling. Sometimes I start by writing a brief description of the incident that is bothering me. Other times I begin by pouring out my feelings. Either way, the process helps me gain clarity as I pull out or externalize what's going on inside of me emotionally. As Patsy Clairmont wrote, "Whether you express your feelings in a poem, a drawing, or a letter, the important benefit of journalizing is that it gives you somewhere besides inside yourself to carry your emotions."[4]

Although some people resist journaling because they believe it is too time consuming, remember that it's far better to explore our emotional aches in writing rather than watch our most precious relationships deteriorate or our physical health decline. The time and resources it would take to restore broken relationships and regain our health can be more costly than the minutes and the money we would expend on paper and pen.

Henri Nouwen, a Catholic priest who authored many books on the deeper side of spiritual living, once spent seven months in a Trappist monastery. *The Genesee Diary,* his account of the experience, reveals how he used journaling to process and identify some of his unpleasant thoughts and feelings:

> Thursday, July 13
>
> My thoughts not only wandered in all directions, but

started to brood on many negative feelings, feelings of
hostility toward people who had not given me the attention I wanted, feelings of jealousy toward people who
received more than I, feelings of self-pity in regard to
people who had not written, and many feelings of regret
and guilt toward people with whom I had strained relationships. While pulling and pushing with the crowbar,
all these feelings kept pulling and pushing in me.[5]

Maybe like me you find comfort in knowing you aren't the only
Christian who struggles with difficult emotions. When we're feeling hounded, we can expose the emotions that surface by writing
about them and naming them, thereby protecting our inner peace.
Five days after his July 13 entry, Nouwen confronted more emotional trash:

Thursday, July 18

I hardly remember what it was, but a small critical remark and a few irritations during my work in the bakery
were enough to tumble me head-over-heels into a deep,
morose mood. Many hostile feelings were triggered and
in a long sequence of morbid associations, I felt worse
and worse about myself, my past, my work, and all the
people who came to mind. But happily I saw myself
tumbling and was amazed how little was needed to lose
my peace of mind and to pull my whole world out of
perspective. Oh, how vulnerable I am!

The milieu of this place full of prayerful people prevents
me from acting out, from getting angry, from bursting
open. I can sit down and see how quickly the little empty
place of peace in my heart is filled again with rocks and
garbage falling down from all sides.[6]

We too are vulnerable to the disquieting thoughts and feelings
that fill our "place of peace." But no matter how rapidly our trash
accumulates, it's encouraging to know journaling gives us a healthy

way of identifying what we're feeling *before* we let it get out of control and harm us or those we love.

One person told me he isn't able to lie to himself when he writes about his feelings and thoughts. If he just talks to others he can put a spin on the incident or on his responses and attitudes. As he writes, he pauses now and then to ask, "What am I thinking that makes me feel this way?" If a belief comes to mind, he writes it down and examines it for truthfulness.

If you've never journaled, start by finding a journal or any composition book or notebook. Choose a place and a time of day where you will have some privacy and be most likely to write. Get comfortable and then just start jotting down what is going on in your life now or about an experience from the past. The most important aspect of this practice is to note how *you feel* about the emotional impact of the event or circumstances. Some days I might jot down only a sentence or two in my journal. Other days, when I'm quite upset, I'll write several pages. In fact, that is what I did as I worked through my jumbled feelings around that conference I co-led with my friend. Journaling enabled me to see that I was being extremely sensitive to criticism and I was feeling manipulated and controlled.

If journaling is uncomfortable for you, pretend you're writing about the experience in an email. One of my closest friends doesn't journal, but she does process what she's struggling with in her emails, which she sometimes sends to me. Recently she wrote, "Actually writing this email was like having a good cry. It gave me the opportunity to look at how I could have been stuck…and realize that it is just my bruised ego that's bothering me." If you do journal emails, make sure you send it to someone who is safe and trustworthy. Or why not send them to yourself? This is safer because you know these personal private emails won't get forwarded to people who might not care about you or would use your words against you in some way.

Another idea is to write a letter to the other people involved in the emotional situation. *But don't mail it.* That might make things worse. In fact, you might want to destroy the letter after you've written it. *The letter is just for you*—to help *you* identify your emotions and what is true in the situation.

Talk with Someone You Trust

Talking to a caring friend, pastor, counselor, or a good listener we trust can help us clarify the issues and find the right words to express our emotions. We want and need people in our lives who will love us and accept us as we are *and* who aren't afraid to tell us the truth. I'm blessed to have several such friends. However, if I ignore what they say, if I'm close-minded to their views, or if I become defensive about my perspective, their wisdom won't help me at all.

Recently I was upset with someone who attacked me verbally. Or at least that's how I perceived it. When I discussed the incident with two people who had witnessed the event, they both told me they thought I was tired at the time and had overreacted. I considered what they said and realized they were right.

TRASH TALK

Treat other people's emotional garbage as garbage. Don't take it personally—it probably has very little to do with you.

RANDY SCHUTT

Talking with others can also be helpful when people unload their stuff on us, and we are left to sort things out. It's like when your neighbor's leaves or trash blows into your yard. It's their garbage, but you are the one who has to clean up the mess. Sometimes discussing with someone else what another person told us (not gossiping!) can be so valuable in helping us process what we're feeling. On another occasion when I was confused about what I was feeling, a wise friend said, "Georgia, this isn't your issue. Just remember some people are better loved at a distance." Although I had to deal with the fallout from the situation, I was able to move on.

Other people, especially the ones who share our values, can help us see what we might be missing. We all have blind spots, so we don't see every situation as it really is. Because of these mental distortions, we can minimize or exaggerate our role in a situation.

In my book *How Not to Date a Loser: A Guide to Making Smart Choices,* I discuss the most common blind spots people have. One of them is that we often focus on a few details or the wrong details and miss the big picture. Another blind spot is caused when we get stuck on past experiences and overreact to current ones, unaware that we're responding to old issues. How many of us, after an emotionally charged event, have only seen our hurts and pain and failed to notice what we said, or did, or how our response hurt others? Talking with someone we trust can help us see what we don't readily see on our own.

Be Physically Active

Moving your body is a great way to sort things out. Walking, jogging, lifting weights, cleaning house, kneading dough, woodworking, carpentry, and digging in the dirt are some physical activities that may enable you to think more clearly.

I'm an avid gardener, and there have been many days where I've been able to dig down to the bottom of what I was feeling as I weeded, pruned, and hoed. A friend of mine shared that one day at her office job she became so upset at a coworker that she couldn't sit still at her desk. She left the building and paced up and down the sidewalk for a few minutes, feeling a jumble of emotions and not being able to get a handle on them. She was ready to explode. Just then she spied a batch of tall weeds in a flowerbed around the corner that must have been overlooked by the groundskeeper. *I might as well make myself useful,* she thought. *If I could only pull out that person like I pull out weeds.* She carefully maneuvered between the bushes so as not to dirty her clothing, bent down, and pulled out the weeds one by one. As she did so she could feel her emotions settling one by one. *Thanks, God. Did you cause these weeds to be left here just for me, for today, because you knew I'd need them?*

Take Time for Rest and Renewal

When our physical and mental resources are exhausted, it can be extremely difficult to accurately discern what we're feeling. Our abilities to read a situation correctly and think clearly may be impaired. If we fail to take the time to rest and replenish our depleted resources, we can get caught in a vicious cycle of listening and considering and heeding the voices and opinions of those around us whether they are true or not.

Sometimes we only need a good night's rest to identify what's going on. Other times we may need more sleep or some time to sit quietly. I know a man who had some hard thinking to do so he "borrowed" a friend's secluded backyard that was bordered by woods. The man spent several days on a lawn chair, resting and relaxing as he watched the birds and small critters. This quiet vacation gave him the clarity he needed to deal with his feelings on an important issue.

Lay Down What You Can't Control

If we have done a good job separating and identifying our emotions, we often come to a point where we need to lay them down. Laying them down can be part of forgiveness, which we'll discuss in more detail in chapters 6 and 7. Sometimes as we process our emotions we may realize we have no control or power to resolve a problem. When there is nothing more we can do, we must let it go. Even though we might want to hold on to it tightly, we need to accept our feelings and the reality of the situation and then acknowledge what we can't change by putting it aside and moving on.

Cheryl used the methods we've discussed to deal with her emotions after unexpectedly losing her job as a nonprofit fund-raiser. As you read her story, imagine her load of emotions getting dumped at the recycling center. They are going through a conveyor belt sorter, where each piece is being separated and processed. Notice how she repeated several methods as new emotions came into her awareness.

> I had so many feelings I didn't know where to begin. I spent the lengthy commute home staring out the window of the train—in shock. How could this happen?

After all, I had written the grant proposal that allowed the nonprofit organization to hire the person who, I now realized, had steadily and stealthily rubbed me out. Why didn't I see it coming? I prayed, thanking God for helping me get through that final meeting without displaying unprofessional emotions. [Cheryl prayed.]

The next few days, my major feeling was overwhelming tiredness. Most mornings I could barely drag myself out of bed, so I allowed myself some extra sleep. I realized I was exhausted from having poured my heart and soul into my work for five years. [She rested.]

While I rested, I had time to talk to God. [She prayed.] I told him I felt used and abused. I asked him if this was all the thanks I was to get for a job well done. I told him I was infuriated at the new hire. I prayed for justice. Gradually I found I could thank God for a few things. [She prayed more.] I thanked him that he had led me to read Proverbs 15:1: "A gentle answer turns away wrath, but a harsh word stirs up anger" the day I was let go. Having that verse fresh in my mind prevented me from saying things in anger to my two bosses that I would have later regretted. Burning one's bridges is never a good idea.

After many times of prayer, I realized I felt guilty. I thought I must have done or not done something that caused me to lose my job. I knew I should open my Bible, but I was afraid of what I might read. A couple of days I just sat and stared at my closed Bible, praying for strength and courage to open it. [She prayed more.] Finally, I decided to trust God. I turned to the books of Psalms and Proverbs and read wherever my Bible fell open. [She read Scripture.] I just read snippets. That's all I could manage.

During these times I often "happened" to read verses about pride or arrogance. "God, did I lose my job because I was proud?" God brought a conversation to my mind where I had talked disrespectfully to one boss. I felt shocked and grieved with myself. I had thought I was so blameless. I realized my heart was proud. I asked God to forgive me. [She prayed again.] I realized I was exceedingly sad.

I became aware that I was carrying a whole batch of emotions. I felt guiltier now than ever that I had caused my job loss. I felt like a failure. I felt like the past five years had been a failure. I felt useless. I felt unneeded and unwanted. I was afraid and worried I would never find another good job. [She used "feeling words" to describe what she was going through.] After job searching for several weeks, I was unable to land even an interview, much less a new job. I felt that I was no good at anything. Crying has always been a stress reliever for me. I spent lots of mornings in the shower, wailing over my heart sin and my situation. [She expressed and released her emotions safely.]

Obviously this path was a downward spiral. It was leading me to Defeat City—a place Satan loves to get Christians trapped. I needed help. Thankfully my Bible-study group had a meeting at the right time. I shared some of my feelings, and my friends set my feet on a better path. [She talked with trusted friends.]

I thanked God that he disciplines his children because he loves us. I asked him to help me become more humble all the time. I used Scripture to pray, asking God to set a watch on my mouth and guard my lips. I asked him to help me forgive and to create something good out of my situation. [She read Scripture and prayed.]

One day I realized I felt hurt and angry at one particular boss and one coworker. Prior to this day I'd thought I'd had held this boss almost blameless and that I'd seen this coworker as a great ally. As I replayed incidents and conversations in my mind, my anger boiled. I vacuumed my carpets with all the vigor of that anger. [She was physically active.]

Of course, throughout the weeks and months as I dealt
with my emotions, I also talked to my husband and two
adult children. [She talked with people she trusted and
who cared about her.] They were a great help. My children reminded me of God's promises—promises I had
preached to them. It was gratifying to know they'd listened.

It's been eight months now. I still haven't found a new
full-time job, but I am emotionally recovered. God is
providing for my needs. I am able to thank him for my
former job and its loss. [She laid down what she couldn't
control.]

God is so good. I have plenty of time now to help other
family members through their own difficulties. I'm still
working at choosing forgiveness of the new hire. I pray for
his wife and six children—that when God exercises justice
he will spare them. I still feel pain when I see the name of
the organization where I worked, but with time the pain
has lessened and continues to diminish. Most of all, I'm
trusting in God, not in a career, paycheck, bank account,
accolades, to-do lists, or even being busy. God takes care
of Cheryl. [She trusted and depended on God.]

Did you notice that handling her emotions in a healthy way was
a process? And sometimes unloading, sorting, and separating our
emotional stuff can make quite a mess? When you are mid-transfor-
mation, there will be moments when you look around and see the
disorder and become overwhelmed, weary, or skeptical. From a distance, this disorganization may resemble the same old dirty mess of
emotions you started with. In fact, it may look even more chaotic.

However, if you look more closely, you'll realize that this mid-
point confusion isn't the same at all. You have made real progress.
Layers of pain, loss, and regret have been removed. Pieces that didn't
fit into a healthy version of your life have been cleared away. You'll
discover there is order to the chaos.

You haven't allowed the feelings of shame and guilt to spread over every aspect of your life. Instead you've related them to a particular occurrence in your life, to unhealthy labels you heard during childhood (such as "bad" or "unworthy"), or from unhealthy adult relationships. You'll soon notice that your once-sharp anger is no longer cutting into your heart or severing your friendships. The jagged edges have been worn down, smoothed by God's mercy, along with our forgiveness of self and others.

TRASH TALK

When life hands you lemons, grind them in
the garbage disposal to replace unpleasant
odors with a fresh lemon scent.

SHARON HANBY-ROBIE AND DEB STRUBEL

Yes, there is still work to be done, wisdom to be gathered, and wounds to be tended. But now the piles you're sifting through are part of your healing process. And as the layers of emotions are sorted and recycled or hauled to the dumpster, you'll feel lighter and more able to deal with what remains.

If panic tries to set back in and life begins to look overwhelming again, stop and pray for the Holy Spirit's leading. Praise God for the work of awareness and healing he's taking you through. And remember to congratulate yourself for a job well done. You aren't hiding from the issues or drowning in a mess of emotions anymore. You're up to the task of ditching the trash. Rejoice in this big step toward a new life approach.

Now that you've separated out the insecurities, fears, anger, and irritations, you are ready to take the next step toward processing them. We'll explore which ones can be recycled, which ones can be composted, and which ones need to be discarded. Let's keep moving forward. You're doing great.

TIME TO TAKE OUT THE TRASH

1. Are you thinking oriented or emotionally oriented? How do you know?

2. When identifying and separating emotions, how can having a trusted friend who is different from you help? How can a friend similar to you help?

3. List some Scriptures that have helped you identify and work through your emotions. If appropriate, share with your group or a trusted friend the before and after circumstances of an emotional incident you've worked through.

4. The next time something or someone irritates you, challenge yourself to write about the incident rather than just talk about it. Be direct and journal exactly how you are feeling. You may want to start your entry by addressing it to God. Then, like David did in the book of Psalms, pour out your raw emotions at God's feet.

4

What Desires Need
to Be Discarded?

Sometimes our legitimate desires become warped by "wrong thinking" that results in emotional garbage weighing us down. Courtney had always wanted to travel. This is a perfectly legitimate desire. When she and Chuck were first married, they frequently traveled to Paris, San Francisco, and other beautiful places. Gradually, as often happens, Chuck became more involved with his work and found it increasingly difficult to get away.

"He knew I loved to experience new places, so he began giving me homemade vouchers for my birthday and Christmas," Courtney shared. "Each note was a promise to take me on a vacation somewhere that I wanted to visit, such as London."

As the years passed, the actual trips became scarce and the notes accumulated. Courtney's resentment grew along with the pile until one Christmas she told him, "Don't give me any more notes as gifts because we never go. I have a jewelry box filled with empty promises."

From then on Chuck would say, "When I retire I promise we'll go to London" or "When I retire we'll go to Hawaii." Courtney lived her days looking forward to Chuck's retirement and their future travels.

Twenty-five years passed.

About a year after Chuck retired, Courtney and I met for lunch. I was surprised that this normally vibrant woman appeared so sad. Her eyes lacked their normal sparkle, and she seemed to be only going through the motions of living. As I gently probed, she resisted sharing any heartaches or difficulties. But I couldn't shake the gnawing feeling that something wasn't right with my friend. Finally, at the end of our lunch, I said, "I've known you for years, and I just have to say I don't know what's going on, but something seems different."

She thanked me for my concern and assured me everything was fine.

For weeks after that lunch, Courtney kept popping into my mind. Each time I prayed for her, asking for God's peace and healing for whatever was plaguing her.

Six months later Courtney and I met for lunch again. As soon as I saw her I noticed the sparkle had returned to her eyes. She was full of life again.

"What happened? You look dramatically different from six months ago," I said.

With a sheepish smile Courtney told me that after our lunch she began praying, asking God to show her what was bothering her. Over several weeks, God revealed the issue. "Chuck had always promised when he retired we would see the world," she said. "But now that he's retired he's consumed with volunteer work and consulting. Oh, we travel some, but nothing like I thought we would." Her voice faded as she glanced down at the table. "That's when the truth hit me," she said. "Chuck will always be busy, and I'm not ever going to be traveling extensively.

"As I prayed, journaled, and read Scripture, God kept bringing me back to Romans 12:2: 'Do not conform any longer to the pattern of this world, but be transformed by the renewing of your mind. Then you will be able to test and approve what God's will is—his good, pleasing and perfect will.' God showed me that there was nothing wrong with my dreams, but unless I changed and renewed my mind, I would continue to be sad and bitter."

"But Chuck promised you those trips!" I blurted. "You waited all your life for those vacations. He needs to take you."

"Georgia, he's not going to change," Courtney said with conviction. "And I'm certainly not divorcing him over this issue. I love Chuck. He's a good man. As hard as it was, I had to let go of what *for me* were unrealistic expectations. That was the only way I could be free to embrace new dreams."

I was speechless. I knew surrendering her desires to travel, especially after all those years of waiting, had to be tough. But I couldn't deny the difference in her. She really was a new person who was excited about her future.

I often share Courtney's story during speaking engagements, and it's amazing how many people identify with her struggle. As one woman said, "That's my story too. I'm not free yet, but I will be."

Unless we are paying attention, we too can get tangled up with our unfulfilled desires. There is nothing wrong with having hopes and dreams. Courtney's desires were reasonable and valid. As her story illustrates, however, some of our tightly held but unrealized or unrealistic longings set us up for disappointment, anger, and despair. And these emotions, if not handled well, will negatively impact our relationships and lives.

I'm not suggesting that it's unrealistic to expect people to follow through on their promises or to be honest and respectful. I'm not suggesting that it is unrealistic for you to expect your spouse to be faithful to you and not harm you physically. What I am suggesting is that we need to be self-aware and understand that some of our relational problems might be caused by our refusal to reevaluate our desires to make sure they're reasonable and what the potential is for their fulfillment.

Understanding the Downward Cycle

Our authentic desires have the capability of subtly, or not so subtly, sending us into a downward cycle. Let me introduce you to Beth. She wanted a larger home with plenty of land to raise horses. However, she and her husband were barely keeping up with the mortgage, bills, and repairs on their current home. Unless her husband took a second job, which could jeopardize his health because of ongoing heart problems, a larger property was out of the question.

But Beth clung to her dream. Before long she convinced herself that a new property was essential to the well-being of her family. Confusing her desire with need, she began to unrealistically expect that in some way her husband would provide a bigger home and more property for her and their children.

When it became apparent that, short of a miracle, her husband wasn't going to fulfill her expectations, Beth became critical and demanding. "You need to do something—like get a better job," she told him repeatedly. "We can't live this way." As the months passed and her husband failed to respond and act according to her demands, she became angry and verbally attacked him. "Sonya's husband has a great paying job and provides lots of things for their family, but on your salary we can barely scrape by. When are you going to step up to the plate, be a man, and make something of your life?"

Beth didn't deal with her emotions in a constructive way, and soon they were in control and damaging her family relationships and happiness.

Beth's story illustrates what happens when we refuse to reexamine and let go of some of our unachieved desires. The root of Beth's problem is a common one for us, and it's outlined in the Bible. James warns us that our desires can battle within us and become demands, which then create conflict and can finally lead to disconnections with people. He wrote, "What causes fights and quarrels among you? Don't they come from your desires that battle within you? You want something but don't get it. You kill and covet, but you cannot have what you want. You quarrel and fight" (James 4:1-2).

John Stringer, a former pastor of mine, described how this principle of "a desire gone bad" is frequently acted out in our relationships:

I desire…

  I need you to…

    I expect you to…

      I demand that you…

        If you fail to fulfill my desire I will punish you by
        either withdrawing from you or attacking you.

Let's visualize this cycle in a different way for added clarity:

Desires

Needs

Expectations

Demands

Disconnections (punishment)

Aggressive/passive
(responding physically by attacking/distancing
or emotionally detaching through silence)

Notice that we are moving in a downward direction, further away from handling emotions in a healthy manner, further away from a positive relationship, and further away from handling the situation in a biblical way. The further we get from Jesus, the more messed up our emotions become, and that means we're generating more emotional trash we'll eventually have to deal with.

We can rid ourselves of desires gone awry at any time by putting them in the trash and leaving them at the curb for the Master Trash Remover to take away. Until we do that, the downward cycle will continue. Pastor Stringer explained that the consequences of staying in the downward spiral is that what we desire takes ownership of our hearts and means more to us than God or the people we care about.

Let's take a closer look at each of the points in the downward cycle.

Desires

A desire is something we long for, hope for, yearn for:

- I desire that my life will make a positive difference in the lives of my family, friends, and others.

- I desire to be married someday.

- I desire to have enough money to pay my bills and live comfortably.

- I desire to be healthy until the day I die and then pass quietly in my sleep.

- I desire a new kitchen to replace the one I have which is 35 years old.

- I desire to eat anything I want and never gain weight.

Recognizing and owning our desires is important. Without knowledge of our deepest longings, we won't be able to discern whether we are holding any of our desires too tightly. We won't notice when something we desire, such as a better car, a new appliance, a raise, a helping hand, an apology, becomes something we think we need.

Needs

It's so easy to confuse what we want with what is really a necessity, a true need. A need, for this discussion, is something we require. For example, water to drink is a need. It is essential to our well-being. Without water we would die. A need can also be reliable transportation to get us to work. Whether we take the bus, the subway, ride with a friend, or have our own vehicle, we are finding ways to fulfill the genuine need of getting to work to earn a living.

In contrast, a distorted, work-related need would be the belief that we need the status of driving a Jaguar to work. Another distorted work need might center on being successful in our careers no matter who gets hurt and what values we have to compromise.

TRASH TALK

Desire divorced from God becomes decadence.
Decadence, in turn, chases away true, godly
pleasure. We have an obligation to preserve
holy pleasure, in part by approaching God with
open, inquiring hands: "May I have this?"

GARY THOMAS

Although we need serviceable shoes, we can twist that need into believing we need a closet stuffed with Christian Louboutin designer shoes or Bruno Magli boots.

Relationally, an emotional need is to have our identity and the foundation of who we are met in Jesus. A distorted need would be to think we must have the approval of specific people. For instance, we may be devastated when our parents don't affirm us or are critical of us.

Before we automatically believe the internal voice that says, "This isn't just a wish; this is a need. I have to have this. It's essential to my health and well-being," reconsider. Ask, "Do I really need this? What will happen to me if I don't get this?" Oswald Chambers said, "If I could look at myself from God's perspective, what would he say are my true needs?" Asking yourself these few defining questions can help clarify the difference between a distorted need and a true need.

We all want to have our desires met. That's normal. And living and dealing with unfulfilled longings is difficult and painful. However, when we fail to recognize that something is a distorted need, we often take the next false step: We expect that desire to be ful-filled.

Expectations

What often propels us in the vicious downward cycle are our unrealistic expectations for ourselves, others, and even for God. For instance, we come to believe we deserve something. Or if we've done something good, we believe we should be rewarded in a certain way. If you recall, Courtney expected that after waiting patiently all those years, her husband, Chuck, would stop his activities and travel with her. Obviously that didn't happen, so she had a choice to make. Was she going to let her expectations go or was she going to be bitter and depressed?

Taking the time to step back and reevaluate can reveal whether you are merely hoping and planning for something to happen or you have become entrenched in something unrealistic. First, pray. Ask God to give you clarity. Then use these questions to sort through your expectations:

- Am I expecting someone to give me the desires of my heart?

- Am I expecting someone to pay me back at a certain time and in a certain way for a favor I did for him or her?

- Am I expecting something from God?

- Am I trusting God for this?

As the wise psalmist said, "My soul, wait silently for God alone, for my expectation *is* from Him" (Psalm 62:5 NKJV).

Another reality of life is that people's expectations often clash. So it's important not to confuse your expectations with the expec-tations of someone else who may be caught in his or her own down-ward cycle. For example, maybe a good friend of yours is making continuous demands for your time and attention when you have clearly explained you are consumed with taking care of your critically ill mother. You've talked to your friend and explained your situation until you are blue in the face, yet she continues to demand more time than you can possibly give. Does this mean you're caught in a downward cycle of demanding or punishing if you choose to distance yourself from her because you can't live up to her expectations? No. The problem isn't *your* unrealistic expectations; the issue is *her* unrealistic expectations. She is choosing to disregard your need for grace and respect regarding the situation with your mother.

But when we're stuck in our own unrealistic expectations and don't get what we hoped for from someone, our next interaction with this person might be infused with our negative attitude. Because we believe it is our right to have our needs met, we blame others for the hurt and pain we are experiencing and start giving ultimatums or withdrawing emotionally.

Demands

As Oswald Chambers warned,

> If we love someone, but do not love God, we demand total perfection and righteousness from that person, and when we do not get it we become cruel and vindictive; yet we are demanding of a human being something which he or she cannot possibly give. There is only one Being who can completely satisfy to the absolute depth of the hurting human heart, and this is the Lord Jesus Christ.[7]

Stacy had been seriously dating Dan for more than a year. A few days before Easter he mentioned that he planned to go to his church that Sunday. He didn't invite her to go along. Stacy said nothing to Dan, but she immediately called her best friend.

"What kind of relationship do you think Dan and I have?" Stacy asked. "He's coming to Easter dinner with my family, so I assumed we'd go to church together. Maybe I'm not all that important to him. If he doesn't invite me to his church or come to mine for Easter, then that's it. I'm going to tell him he can forget my going to his dear brother's birthday party!"

Stacy expectation was that in a serious relationship, she and her boyfriend would go to Easter services together. Stacy wanted to be with Dan. She had the unrealistic expectation that Dan could read her mind and know how important going together to church on Easter was to her. And she was willing to demand he go with her or else she would retaliate by not going to his brother's party as planned.

Like Stacy, we often expect those around us to read our minds and know our hopes and desires, possibly because we assume they desire the same things. We expect that others will meet our desires, whether they are realistic or not. We want what we want in our time and in our way. Doesn't this sound familiar? We all have this tendency.

Punishment and Disconnections

Making demands of others can also be a way we attempt to control them. When our desires aren't met, things can quickly escalate. We are often tempted to react as Stacy started to do—demanding our way or else: "You failed to do what I wanted, so I'm not going to do what you want."

When retaliation enters our minds, it doesn't advance our cause of getting our needs met. In fact, it erodes our relationships. Retaliation can be passive—we withdraw from the scene or refuse to talk to the particular person. We hope they suffer by our silence. Or maybe our style is to be more aggressive. We attack verbally or by our actions. Whatever the approach, the bottom line looks like this: "You didn't do what I wanted or expected, so I'm going to punish you by not doing what you want or expect." Convinced our feelings are justified, in our minds our desires become needs that we expect to be met. We could even look at them as "little gods" that are demanding their due.

If we don't give ourselves the gift of time and reflection to examine our attitudes and actions to make sure we're keeping our needs and our desires clear, we may give up on other people and discard relationships like dead batteries that can't be recharged. We then look to other ways or other people to get our demanding desires met. This approach never works for long. As we are reminded in Psalm 16:4, "The sorrows of those will increase who run after other gods." Unless we turn to God, taking our longings to him and trusting him, it's only a matter of time until we get to the place where we start the vicious cycle all over again with another person or with another situation. Our unfulfilled desires once again will battle within us.

Psychologist and author Dan Allender wrote:

> When we demand that another person provide safety, certainty, and fulfillment of our deepest desires, we turn from God to an idol for the fulfillment of our needs.
>
> When we turn from God, we inevitably demand of others the very things we miss in our relationship with God. If we don't know his deep care and protection, then we will insist another human being provide what we lack.[8]

How to Reverse the Downward Cycle

The vicious downward cycle can be broken and reversed. It's not always easy, but we can identify and discard those desires that get corrupted *before* they harm or destroy our relationships. What is the process that enables us to break free and avoid hurting ourselves and others?

- Recognize when a desire has become a need, expectation, or demand.

- Grieve the hurts and disappointments of unmet expectations.

- Embrace reality or "what is."

Recognize When a Desire Has Become a Need, Expectation, or Demand

Recently I decided to iron a white blouse. As the iron heated up, it started spitting out brown water. I pressed the steam button, and it continued to spit out more dirty water. Finally, after several minutes, it cleaned itself out and the steam became clear. At that point I safely ironed my blouse without staining it. Since I don't put brown water into my iron, I assumed sediment had built up inside, causing the water to turn brown. This isn't the first time that has happened over the years, so now I check the burst of steam to see if it is clear before I iron.

Similarly, our desires can be relatively pure, but in our hearts we have a buildup of "sediment." We can call this our sin nature. Our legitimate desires become contaminated and corrupted. As a result, what comes out of our hearts is impure and harmful to what is good in our lives. Knowing that we have hurt our relationships in the past by our "contaminated" desires, we want to be alert and quickly identify when a desire is going or has gone "bad." One way to do this is by increasing our "expectation awareness." Through prayer and paying attention to our thoughts, words, and actions, we will be less likely to become ensnared by the way we think our world should be. Here is a sampling of what may signal that we're holding unrealistic expectations:

- I assume people I interact with will always be kind, grateful, and polite.

- I'm depressed when my new computer has major problems or slows down for no apparent reason after only two months.

- I'm frustrated when I have to wait 10 minutes in the express lane at the grocery store.

- I'm irritated when someone at the bank is helped before me even though I arrived first.

- I'm moody when I'm late for an appointment because of traffic.

- I get angry when someone cuts me off in traffic.

- I get depressed when it rains or snows on my days off work.

- I believe I should be able to do something today as well as I could years ago.

- I'm completely drained when I don't meet the high standards I've set.

Awareness of our expectations is key, but even more important is knowing what we think and what we feel about what we desire. For example, Courtney was elated at the thought of traveling to different countries with her husband and devastated when it didn't happen. Because we have feelings attached to our thoughts and desires, identifying our feelings can help us uncover why we often react with intensity when our desires aren't fulfilled.

When Stacy, who was disappointed her boyfriend didn't invite her to Easter service, stopped and reflected on her thoughts and feelings, she realized she believed that being in a serious relationship meant spending holidays together. When she asked herself if she really *needed* Dan to attend church with her on Easter Sunday, she recognized the answer was no. She went further and asked herself if her desire to go to Easter service together meant more to her than her relationship with God or with Dan. Again the answer was no. While she would be extremely disappointed if Dan didn't invite her to join him at church on Easter, she *chose* not to expect he would. She acknowledged that she had initially made an *assumption* rather than expressing her desire or expectation to Dan.

Once she recognized that she'd allowed an unspoken desire to become distorted into a need, she could respond differently. Rather than trying to control Dan by demanding they go to church together or by threatening him with punishment, she decided to talk with him about how she felt. When Stacy shared how important it was to her that they go to church together, Dan changed his plans. Even if he hadn't been willing, the important fact was that Stacy had already made the decision not to wreck their relationship over whatever decision he made.

When we state our expectations, sometimes they will be met and sometimes they won't. When Courtney identified her deep sadness over her husband's unwillingness to follow through and travel extensively, she recognized that if she continued to allow the problem to rule her she would remain unhappy, which would eventually ruin her marriage. Though Courtney was willing to discuss it with Chuck, in contrast to Dan's situation, Chuck never decided to change his plans or schedule. Courtney chose to let her desire go.

Even when we identify what desires are taking control of us and remember that Christ is the only one "who can completely satisfy," that doesn't mean it's easy to let go and move on, especially when what we desire is something that was promised to us. Before we are ready to move forward and embrace new dreams, we may need to grieve over what no longer can be.

Grieve the Hurts and Disappointments of Unmet Expectations

If we have no expectations, we won't be disappointed. That makes sense on the surface, but the reality is that we all have expectations. Simply identifying that we are clinging to an expectation and then letting go of it works for the daily irritations of waiting in line at the grocery store or sitting in a traffic jam. But how do we let go of our expectations *and* the hurt and ramifications that sometimes come when something is extremely important to us?

Hailey, a friend of mine, expected cards from her kids for Mother's Day. But she didn't get anything from her daughter except an empty promise that she would get her a card later. Even though Hailey knew her adult daughter was going through a tough time emotionally, Hailey had invested so much time and energy helping her daughter in the last year that without the Mother's Day card she felt unacknowledged and unappreciated.

Hailey asked me, "How do I let go of my disappointment about not getting a card this year without expecting her to make it up to me next year?"

TRASH TALK

We do not always get what we want, but that doesn't mean that we no longer want. It means we stay awake to the unmet longing and ache. Wait there. Invite Jesus to come there.

JOHN AND STASI ELDRIDGE

The first step for Hailey is to grieve over what didn't happen. Grieving requires acknowledging that you are hurt or disappointed and allowing yourself the time to be upset, whether that means crying, reflecting, praying, writing out your thoughts, or talking through your feelings. Just as you tend to a broken arm, you need to give your disappointments and pain the care and attention they require to heal.

Acknowledging and grieving our hurt and pain enables us to let go and discard what can't happen and what no longer can be so we can be free to accept reality. (We'll explore grief more in chapter 8.)

Embrace Reality or "What Is"

It's difficult to look beyond what we expect and want to happen to see what is good and right and positive about what is. Seeing what's wrong in our lives is so much easier. Therefore, we need to intentionally make the choice to find something good in our current situation. Learning to be grateful for what we have rather than focus on what we didn't get enables us to move beyond our frustrations and irritations toward joy. In Hailey's situation, she focused on the fact that her daughter was normally a kind and considerate person. Courtney focused on the fact that she loved her husband and they had a good marriage instead of dwelling on not traveling.

If Beth, who wanted more land and a bigger house, focused on the blessings of having a caring, hardworking husband and three wonderful children, she would be better able to accept and even embrace the here and now. She'd be happier—and she'd be easier to live with.

Embracing "what is" means rethinking what we *thought* we needed. Embracing our actual circumstances means accepting that people are flawed and life is not always the way we think it ought to be. Living "what is" means putting our trust in God instead of people and things. (I'm not talking about accepting abusive or destructive relationships here. Those need to be taken care of immediately so everyone is safe and stays safe.) In Psalm 16:2 we are reminded about our dependence on Jesus: "Apart from you [LORD,] I have no good thing." Embracing "what is" means we understand that no relationship, child, house, job, or career can satisfy us or be more important to us than God.

As my friend Stephen Weaver at Sandy Cove Ministries often reminds people, "Maybe when things don't go the way we want, we need to fix the way *we thought* they should be." How do we do that? How do we keep from getting stuck in our perceptions of things? We can begin by praying, "Create in me a new, clean heart, O God, filled with clean thoughts and right desires" (Psalm 51:10 TLB). This is recognizing and acknowledging that *only* God knows what is best for us.

While we *think* we know what will bring us joy, happiness, and a meaningful life, research has shown otherwise. Harvard psychologist Daniel Gilbert states that various studies have proven we can't predict what will make us happy. Nor can we accurately forecast how bad or how good something will make us feel. Why? Because we base those predictions on how we feel now. Dr. Gilbert explains that we are often wrong in our projections because "when we imagine future circumstances, we fill in details that won't really come to pass and leave out details that will. When we imagine future feelings, we find it impossible to ignore what we are feeling now and impossible to recognize how we will think about the things that happen later."[9]

Unless we are willing to give up our desires and what we believe we need to be happy, our emotions will take us on roller coaster rides. We will be up when our desires and expectations are met and down—way down—when they aren't.

On the other hand, when we discard those desires, expectations, and demands that have become idols, we are free to experience God's plans and desires for our lives. We are free to live in the here-and-now with peace and joy. Who among us doesn't desire that?

TIME TO TAKE OUT THE TRASH

Many of us have witnessed relationships where a spouse or friend refused to do one small thing, such as go to a special event. The seemingly over-the-top reaction was "That's it! I want nothing to do with this person," "The marriage is over," or "I'm done with this friendship." Part of the problem is that many times we've allowed our resentments to build, sometimes for years, and our frustrated desires send us downward.

1. *Desires:* Before we can determine if we're holding tightly to unrealistic expectations, we need to understand what we desire. What are your hopes and dreams? What do you long for? Children? Grandchildren? To live in a warmer climate? To lose 50 pounds? Rather than bury your hopes deep within, make a list of what you desire. If figuring out what you desire is difficult, think of it as a wish list.

2. *Needs:* Realizing that sometimes we confuse our desires with a distorted need, go through the list you created for question 1 and write *D* for desire and *N* for a true need after each entry.

3. *Expectations:* Examine each entry you identified in question 2 as a desire. Ask, "How am I thinking about it? Am I *hoping* it will

be met or are am I *expecting* or *demanding* that it be met?" Circle any desires that have become expectations or demands.

4. *Demands:* When our expectations aren't met, we can go to great lengths to demand that others fulfill our desires. Are there any expectations you are clinging to and refusing to get rid of? If so, what's keeping you from releasing them and surrendering them to God? What is keeping you from praying, "Lord, I realize I may never get what I expect or want. I give up not only my desires but the demands I put on others. Let your desires fill my heart and shape my life"?

5. *Embrace "what is":* Thinking about the desires you circled and the unmet expectations that may need to be grieved, how can you embrace reality?

6. Write down four things you can be thankful for today.

5

Are You Recycling Your Anger?

Georgia has the energy of three people," my mom's friends said when I was a child. "She's a real tomboy with a will of iron." Yes, I was a strong-spirited little girl who loved to run and get dirty. "Hyperactive" is the term used today. I recall that whenever my grandmother kept me, I would spend as much time as possible racing around her backyard, digging in the dirt, and climbing the tree outside my grandfather's garage. Those times were often interrupted with Grandmother's reminders: "Georgia, tuck in your blouse. Little girls keep their blouses tucked in!" Sometimes I obeyed my grandmother and dutifully tucked my blouse inside my shorts or pants. Other times I just kept running, pretending I didn't hear her.

One day I guess I hit my limit. Grandmother was out on the second-floor balcony hanging up wet laundry while I was playing in her bedroom. "Georgia," Grandmother said, "tuck in your blouse. Little girls are to look nice and not have their blouses hanging out."

Instead of obeying, I slammed the door between the balcony porch and her bedroom, which automatically locked, trapping my grandmother outside.

"Georgia, please open the door," she demanded. "I can't climb down from the second floor."

At first her pounding and pleading had no effect on me. Hands firmly on my five-year-old hips, I was making a statement. My body was saying, "Let me be me! I don't like having to tuck in my blouse! It makes me mad!"

Minutes later I changed my mind, but my little fingers couldn't move the rusty latch. That's when I knew I was in big trouble. I wanted to run from the scene.

Grandmother climbed over the railing and down the treacherous 10-foot support post. She made it to the ground hollering, "Georgia, you are a bad girl! What kind of child would lock her grandmother on a balcony?"

While in that instance, I did treat my grandmother badly, I realize now that my poor behavior didn't make me a "bad person." But at that age my mind wasn't able to make that distinction. My young self equated my five-year-old fury with my grandmother's words about being bad. After that incident whenever I felt angry, I believed the lie that I was a bad person and felt shame. And since I didn't want to be a bad person, for years I rarely admitted to times of anger. I often wonder how my life would have been different if someone in my early years had taught me the skills to express my anger constructively. It would have been even better if someone had taught me that anger can be useful—even recycled.

Recognize and Admit Your Anger

The first step in recycling anger is to recognize and admit we feel angry. Many of us believe, as I did, that being angry is wrong. Because we haven't learned how to express this powerful emotion in constructive ways, our angry feelings make us uncomfortable. Rather than differentiating between destructive and constructive ways to express anger, we try to deny or ignore the negative feelings. We attempt to minimize or hide these feelings by calling them other names, for instance, "I'm not angry, I'm just upset." Or we separate ourselves from the feelings by staying busy or distracting ourselves.

=========================== **TRASH TALK** ===========================

*Feelings buried alive never die!...*They will make
themselves known when you least expect it.
KAROL K. TRUMAN

One of my coaching clients shared an emotionally painful experience, totally unaware that her fists were tightly clenched while she sat across the table from me and talked.

"That must have made you feel really angry," I commented.

"No, not at all," she said as she made one snide, cutting remark after another about the person who had hurt her.

After several minutes she stopped and said, "You are very perceptive to pick up how angry I felt."

I didn't need a degree in psychology to take note of the obvious anger signs she exhibited. Like many of us, she had been punished as a child for getting angry. She was never taught how to handle strong emotions, so she made every attempt to distance herself from them.

No matter how hard we strive to be kind, loving, compassionate people, the truth is we all experience anger and we all struggle at times with controlling our anger. One common area that generates anger is driving. If we haven't done it ourselves, we all know people who honk or curse at other drivers they think are bad or rude drivers. And if they choose not to be verbal, they often wave their fists or arms or make obscene gestures.

Getting a grip on our anger begins with recognizing that it is a God-given emotion. Everyone gets angry, but that doesn't mean we have to get trapped in unhealthy patterns of anger behavior or denial.

Avoid Expressing Anger Destructively

There are at least six major ways we can express our anger in a harmful manner.

Aggressive Action

Aggression is the outward expression we most often identify with anger. Shoving, slapping, hitting, and kicking are common physical responses. We may throw things or break items that belong to us or others. We can be verbally aggressive by yelling, name-calling, insulting, or cursing.

Recently I watched a movie where two adversaries began their aggressive battle by shouting obscenities at each other. Then they jabbed each other with their fingers. They escalated their heated argument by wrestling each other to the ground. Finally some bystanders pulled them apart, but they continued their verbal attacks.

This kind of behavior fuels the conflict and makes us the target of more intense anger. Scripture says, "Anger boomerangs. You can spot a fool by the lumps on his head" (Ecclesiastes 7:9 MSG).

Critical Words

Verbal attacks and being critical may seem similar, but criticism isn't always as obvious. Delivered politely without using a loud voice or foul language can make it very subtle. Some experienced criticizers deliver their verbal jabs while smiling and end by saying, "I'm only telling you this for your own good." Sometimes we're not even sure we're being criticized because it's veiled so carefully.

Criticism, as a destructive expression of anger, is finding fault or expressing disapproval of another person. I remember overhearing a husband criticize his wife as we all waited in line at the grocery store. He berated everything about her, from the outfit she had on to the meal she had cooked the evening before. He finished his tirade by saying, "You never think about anyone but yourself."

His anger had an infectious quality. It spread to me, and I became irritated just listening to him. I wanted to lash out at him with a caustic comment about his behavior but, like his wife, I said nothing.

Relationship expert John Gottman was able to predict with 94 percent accuracy which of more than 200 couples would get a divorce within three years. Like the husband at the grocery store, Dr. Gottman found that criticism filled with contempt was very destructive to the health of a marriage [or any relationship]. The person receiving these comments feels "ashamed, disliked, blamed, and defective—all of which are more likely to lead to a defensive response than to steps to improve things."[1]

Vengeful Behavior

"I'll get even with him," Abby said after her husband left her to be with someone else. "He's not going to get away with this."

The desire to get back at someone is a common reaction when we've been hurt or violated. After I shared the story of what I did to my grandmother, one person sheepishly shared, "When I was about five-years-old I was so mad at my older sister that I took the basket filled with her paper dolls and pooped in it. Then I hid the basket so she wouldn't know what I'd done. However, after a few days the smell gave me away."

While we might laugh at our childhood stories now, it's amazing how we, as adults, continue to come up with creative ways to even the score with someone who has hurt us and made us furious. The huge downside is that as long as we focus on getting even we create more problems for ourselves and continue to be weighed down by resentment and bitterness.

Sarcastic Remarks

"I was only kidding" is a comment we often hear after someone has made a cutting remark and we are pulling out the knife and tending to our emotional wound. Sarcastic people seem to enjoy embarrassing others. They may even tell us we are too sensitive if we respond to their jabs. They may defend themselves by saying, "I didn't mean anything by it. Can't you take a joke?"

Sarcastic people are usually angry about something but they don't know it. Making a joke at the expense of others or poking fun at others' sensitive areas—such as age, weight, or hair loss—is using anger to impact others negatively. Sarcastic comments and putdowns do nothing to improve relationships. In fact, they can destroy one, whether quickly or slowly.

Withdrawing Communication

Temporarily leaving the scene of a heated argument can be a good thing. In the midst of conflict it can give both parties an opportunity to calm down and think the issue through. But distancing ourselves becomes destructive when we do it to avoid communicating with someone. People who withdraw often refuse to answer emails or calls—sometimes for days, weeks, or years.

One couple I knew could best be described as icebergs silently passing each other. They communicated only about essential things and never talked about any of the issues that infuriated them. The silence, of course, never resolved anything. Eventually they divorced.

After I gave a talk about anger and "the silent treatment," one woman came up and thanked me. She said, "You know, I've been married for 32 years, and I never thought of myself as being angry when I refuse to talk to my husband or son. I realize now that's exactly how I am feeling. I guess I just didn't want to think of myself as ever getting angry."

Another woman told me, "When I'm furious I shut down and avoid others by getting very busy."

Pouting is another form of withdrawing. Most of us are familiar with the scenario when someone gets upset because things didn't go his or her way; the person sticks out his or her lower lip, goes to the bedroom, slams the door, and sulks. Maybe as a child people learned that this style of cold anger enabled them to manipulate a situation to their advantage. As adults, however, this immature behavior isn't cute, and sulking can be detrimental to relationships.

Withholding Something

Maybe we don't give someone the silent treatment, but we get stingy with our time, attention, money, and other resources. We hold back the very thing we know someone wants or needs.

Cayden is extremely giving of his time and money. Whenever possible he finds ways to help his stay-at-home wife. However, she always knows when he is upset with her. She says, "He'll 'forget' to do something like replace the burned-out brake light on my car. But he'll never admit he is angry. This upsets me, and then I'll withhold my affection and attention in other ways." This kind of vicious downward cycle can lead to fractured marriages.

TRASH TALK

Satan can only plant feelings of envy, fear, bitterness,
or hatred where there is dirt and trash for them
to grow. Clear out the garbage and there will be
no place for these negative feelings to grow.

PENNY OLIVIERI

Did you recognize yourself in any of those descriptions? Once at a women's conference I asked the group which destructive expression of anger they resorted to the most. One of the girls laughed and responded, "All of them!" Whether we use sarcasm, criticism, or withdrawal, we need to recognize that we're turning to harmful and hurtful ways of expressing anger.

Reduce Before You Recycle

The phrase "reduce and recycle" has become popular today with "going green." The idea is not only to recycle more of our trash but also to decrease the number of items that enter the waste stream. In the same way, instead of becoming even more emotional and allowing our anger to escalate, we want to find ways to control the intensity of our anger. We want to learn how to contain our feelings so we can reduce the number of times we "lose it."

Praying, journaling, talking with a close friend, meditating, working out, trusting God to right the wrongs, and simply accepting the injustice of the situation are ways we can reduce our anger. You may need to experiment to find which ways work best for you. Be careful as you experiment. Some methods, such as talking with friends, may make you feel angrier. Let's look at some other strategies that may work for us.

Hit Pause

Before you let loose with a barrage of angry words, hit an imaginary pause button, take several deep breaths, and count to 10. There are many verses in Scripture that support the wisdom of slowing our anger responses:

- Everyone should be quick to listen, slow to speak and slow to become angry (James 1:19).

- A man's wisdom gives him patience; it is to his glory to overlook an offense (Proverbs 19:11).

- Do not be quickly provoked in your spirit, for anger resides in the lap of fools (Ecclesiastes 7:9).

- He who is slow to anger is better than the mighty (Proverbs 16:32 NASB).

- Short-tempered people do foolish things (Proverbs 14:17 NLT).

Taking a moment to stop and think enables us to consider our response rather than immediately lashing out. In the heat of the moment, it can be extremely difficult to turn off anger. I like what one young mother models for her children. She told me, "I give my children timeouts. I tell them sometimes Mommy needs a timeout too so I can pray and think things through." I've heard of another mom who said she "gives herself timeouts so there are no blackouts."

One mother told me she has a sign on her refrigerator with a red light on one side and a green light on the other side. When she turns it to the side showing the red light, it is a visual reminder to be cautious, slow down, and stop before she gets too angry. "I don't want to destroy my children with the Mack truck of my emotional fury."

I read an article recently about how counting to 10 enabled one woman to avoid many of the arguments that her anger-induced reactions used to get her into. "One day at the hospital where I worked as a registered nurse, I went into a patient's room for the first time. Her husband was there and proceeded to throw an angry fit and swear at me. I took a moment and politely said, 'I can see you're really having a difficult time; I'll come back when you're ready.' Later this man apologized for his poor behavior." The nurse said, "Taking 10 and not 'biting the hook' has allowed me to change my attitude and behavior."[2]

Hitting pause gives us time to ask these important questions:

- Is what I'm about to do or say the best for me and for those around me?

- Will I be making the situation worse or better?

- How can I give voice to my feelings, rather than stuff them, in such a way that is helpful rather than harmful?

- How can I respond so I don't fuel the anger of another person?

- What can I do to respond in a godly manner that demonstrates "a gentle answer turns away wrath, but a harsh word stirs up anger" (Proverbs 15:1)?

Monitor Your Thoughts

Pay attention to what you say to yourself because some thoughts are anger-provoking. They have the same effect as pouring gasoline on a fire. Ask, "What am I thinking that makes me feel this way?"

Years ago I was quite upset with a person I worked with. "Paula" continually snapped at me, failed to give me important messages, and intentionally undermined my projects. What made this problem so annoying was that she was especially sweet and kind to another colleague. One minute she growled, telling me she didn't have time to discuss a pressing issue, and the next minute I'd see her helping my colleague with something that could have easily waited. The contrast between how she behaved toward me and how she dealt with the other person was obvious to others in my department too.

One day after she really ticked me off, I started thinking, *If she snaps at me one more time, I'm going to let her have it.*

A few days later she was extremely irritated with me about something insignificant, but in the next moment she was syrupy sweet with the other person. That is when I did just what I'd told myself I would do. I let her have it: "I'm sick and tired of how unprofessional you are. And whatever I've ever done to offend you, I'm sorry." Then I stormed out of her office, adding in a loud voice, "You need to know I no longer want to be treated like a second-class citizen!"

While in the short-term she was more polite to me, over the long-term it didn't make any difference. What is funny...and sad... is that *I* was the one who publicly lashed out and ranted and raved about her actions. *I'm* the one who looked unprofessional. *I* was the one who made a scene at work. And my outburst started with one anger-provoking thought: *If she does this one more time, I'm going to let her have it.*

How much different and less harmful it would have been if I'd prayed to God for help and insights instead of telling myself that I should—even deserved!—to snap if she repeated her behavior toward me.

If you realize you are repeating something to yourself that ignites your rage, reframe the thought into something positive. Think of a phrase that helps you douse your fury. I could have said, "Georgia, be the bigger person here. Don't let her get under your skin." If you're having difficulty figuring out how to reframe your thoughts, ask a trusted friend or counselor for help.

Remember Successful Strategies

When tension rises, think about times when you were angry but didn't explode or do something regrettable. What contributed to your successful self-control? See if you can repeat that strategy and gain control.

Praying and journaling help me dilute my fury. One day I was battling the insurance company over medical bills. I wrote in my journal:

> I can't concentrate on anything. I can't relax. I'm just furious. I continue to battle over medical bills. Today I spent hours attempting to resolve the issue and was repeatedly put on hold. It seems that each time I get a different person with a different answer. Lord, please help me with these intense emotions!

The less intense our anger, the less likely we will lose our temper. It's much harder to gain self-control when the pressure has built up to the point where we blow like an active volcano, spewing red-hot lava everywhere.

Blow off steam safely. Run around the block, lift weights, beat a pillow, hoe the garden or flowerbeds, mow the grass with a push mower, or whatever positive activity gets your heart pumping and shifts your thoughts. If you can't think of anything to do that's useful, at the least choose to do something that will not harm any person or possession.

Identify Who or What Drives You Crazy

No matter how great a day you're having or how good your mood is, there may be one person or situation that can quickly sour your disposition. For Lexi it was her ex-husband's wife. Lexi was planning a family celebration for her son's sixth birthday. Her son,

Ethan, was with her second husband, and she had two daughters with her first husband. Knowing her first husband and his new wife were taking her daughters for a weeklong summer vacation around Ethan's birthday, Lexi asked two months ahead of time when they were returning so she could set the date for her son's party. It was important to her that her son's half-sisters be present. Lexi was told they would return on a Saturday night. Therefore, she planned the family event for the following Sunday.

About three weeks later, after all the arrangements for the party had been confirmed, her ex-husband's wife called to inform her they weren't going to return from their trip until late Sunday night.

Lexi was furious. "I knew it!" she said to her husband after she got off the phone. "She loves to ruin my plans. Why does she always do this to me?"

Fortunately Lexi has come to realize what she was doing to herself. She was allowing the former wife to stress her out:

> Once I understood this. I could learn to accept her as she is. Before I would just shake and sob or fume for days. I was an emotional mess. Now when I start to get angry with her, I remind myself, "You know who she is, and you aren't going to change her."
>
> Actually, I have to tell you she was the best thing that ever happened to me. I would get so upset that she drove me right to God. I learned that when I allow God to handle things, he will—often by working on me. But if I hold on to my anger, nothing happens. I just get angrier and angrier. And then I wake up in the middle of the night furious.

We all have a few triggers that can set us off rather quickly. Being aware of them can put us on the path to reacting differently. Whether we learn to accept things as they are or change our responses like Lexi did, we are taking the responsibility to minimize the intensity of our anger to lessen any subsequent fallout.

Recycle Anger Constructively

While we might understand how rage can fuel more tension in relationships, we aren't always clear on *how* to use it as a helpful source of energy. The goal is not to get rid of anger, but to take that raw energy and turn it into something new, different, and constructive. Converting our anger into a positive force is a lot like recycling plastic containers.

Once our recycled plastics are sorted and cleaned at a recycling center, they are often compressed, tied into bales, and shipped to another location. There the plastic is shredded and then melted into small pellets. These pellets are sent to different manufacturers who make new plastic products. The plastic pellets become warm fleece jackets, different plastic containers, and plastic parts—something fresh and different. The plastic, however, is the *same* raw material from the beginning of the recycling process to the end.

TRASH TALK

Consider how much more you often suffer
from your anger and grief, than from those very
things for which you are angry and grieved.

MARCUS ANTONIUS

In the same way, we can take the energy of our anger and channel it into new, healthy directions. It can be the fuel we need to right a wrong that was done to us or someone we love. It can be the source of energy we use to find solutions to old problems rather than create new ones.

Choose to Make Recycling a Habit

The first step in constructively handling our aggravations involves a decision. *We have to decide to recycle our anger.* While this may seem like an obvious step, until we make the decision we will never change.

When I first began to recycle many years ago I had to stick to my commitment until it became a habit. Choosing to recycle also meant I needed a large plastic receptacle or something that would hold the items until I took them to the collection site. I remember times when it seemed so much easier to toss the plastic and cardboard with the other trash rather than store them until I could haul them to the recycling center. But I made the extra effort because it was important to me. Recycling is now such a habit that I barely have to think about it. And today my recyclables are picked up weekly at the curb. I still need to temporarily store them; they still need to be contained. I don't just toss them out on the street.

Similarly, our goal is not to remove anger from our lives. Anger can be a valuable source of information and energy. We want to recognize our fury, acknowledge it, contain it, and recycle it in a way that is healthier for us and others. Commitment is needed to make any new response a habit. Change isn't always easy, and sometimes this choice may seem impossible or overwhelming. Sheila Walsh, in her book *Honestly,* discusses her struggle:

> My first taste of anger—from my father to me as a child—had affected my whole life. I would do anything I could to diffuse an angry situation. Angry words or tone of voice—spoken even by myself—seemed to me to signal something drastic about to happen. I never gave myself permission to be angry; when things happened in my life that I should have been angry about, I just stuffed the feelings down, ground my teeth and clenched my fists and said nothing. Occasionally, when I wasn't being vigilant, little bits would escape, leaking out in sudden outbursts or sarcasm.[3]

Through the help of professional counselors, Shelia was able to give herself permission to be angry. She wrote, "When I feel myself getting angry now, I take a step back. I go into another room by myself, sit at the Shepherd's feet, and I tell him what I am feeling."

When anger has had a devastating effect on our lives or we lose our temper frequently, we may need the help of a professional counselor. Whether we need help in controlling our rage, giving ourselves permission to admit and express our anger, or learning new ways to deal with it, we must first *make the commitment to change.*

Choose How You Will Recycle

I recently heard Dr. Charles Stanley on an In Touch Ministries broadcast say that anger in the right direction, at the right time, and for the right purpose can be a strong and powerful force. Anger can inspire us to channel our hurt, pain, and fury in a good direction so that ultimately we make a positive difference in the world. He's right. MADD [Mothers Against Drunk Driving] is a good example of how this can happen. Candy Lightner's teenage daughter was killed by a drunk driver. When the repeat offender was given leniency, the outraged Candy promised herself to use her daughter's death for something positive. She organized MADD, which has brought great awareness to the problem of driving under the influence and has saved many lives.

Too many people who face devastating situations like Candy's allow themselves to remain bitter and resentful when they could take their anger and do something to make the lives of others better. Sometimes we get stuck in our anger, and it's a struggle to gain control. But the longer we hold on, the harder it can be to let go.

Let's look at some ideas for redirecting anger into something positive. Some of these suggestions you've seen in other chapters. They work well when modified for various situations.

- *Do something physical.* Any activity that requires physical exertion is helpful and can help dissipate wrath: take a brisk walk, clean the house, cook, bake, knead dough, pound nails.

- *Pray, reflect, and meditate.* Pray for God's guidance. Ask him to show you how to express your anger constructively: "Lord, how do you want me to respond to this?" or "Lord, I'm furious about what he did. What do you want me to do with this anger?"

- *Write in a journal.* Journals are safe places to unload toxic thoughts—sort of like dumping trash in the garbage can. As you write you'll begin to shed your deep hurts and irritations, leaving you with less to recycle. Make sure you keep your journal in a secure place.

- *Share your feelings.* Whether you talk to a counselor or a caring friend, a good listener can help you identify your feelings, sort out what's going on, and express your aggravation constructively.

- *Get rest, eat well, and set priorities.* If every little thing is annoying you, it's time for some rest and pampering. It's amazing how much smaller problems appear after a great meal and a good night's sleep.

Embrace Setbacks

In spite of our best intentions, there will always be times when we "lose it" and act on our anger inappropriately. Recently a close friend commented on something I said and assumed the worst about me. I was hurt and immediately got defensive and angry. That evening I kept replaying what she'd said that hurt me. Each time I went over the scenario, I became angrier. I knew holding on to my anger wasn't the mature and godly way to deal with the situation, but I didn't want to let it go. *After all,* I told myself, *who wouldn't feel this way?*

The next morning I realized how tired I had been the day before and how my lack of sleep had contributed to my overreaction. I still was having trouble letting go though. During my morning devotions I reread some of the verses that talk about handling anger. I wrote in my journal all the traits a wise person possesses when it comes to anger. My list of practical, biblical helps for managing anger keeps growing. In my journal I included my paraphrase in parentheses.

Wise people...

- are quick to hear (listen immediately)—James 1:19.

- are slow to speak (don't get defensive right away)—James 1:19.

- are slow to anger (don't fly off the handle)—Proverbs 19:11.

- are tenderhearted (are not hard-hearted or holding on to grudges)—Ephesians 4:32.

- are forgiving (get rid of bitterness)—Ephesians 4:31-32.

- use self-control (instead of venting everything)—Proverbs 29:11.

- are quick to resolve their anger (don't hold on to it for days and weeks)—Leviticus 19:18.

- stay away from angry people (avoid those who are like time bombs)—Proverbs 22:24-25.

- give a soft answer (don't give a harsh, angry retort)—Proverbs 15:1.

- are quick to overlook a transgression (aren't resentful)—Proverbs 19:11.

After studying this list I realized I still had plenty of room for growth. I wrote a prayer asking God for his forgiveness and help as it was obvious in this situation I was having problems containing my anger. The next day my friend and I talked about the situation. We each apologized for our parts in the tiff and expressed how important our relationship was.

When you've lost your temper and allowed it to rule you, you might find it helpful to write about how you were feeling and what you were thinking about *before* the incident as best as you can remember. Then write about what happened and how you responded. Jot down a prayer asking God for his wisdom and forgiveness. Find a Scripture verse that speaks to you, such as "Fools vent their anger, but the wise quietly hold it back" (Proverbs 29:11 NLT). Imagine yourself holding back the anger like you would restrain a dog that wanted to attack someone. If you are still tempted to attack another person, imagine what would happen to your relationship if this vicious dog was unleashed. Imagery can be powerful, and writing may help you be more purposeful and prayerful in your future responses.

Once we experience the benefits of taking time to redirect our frustrations and irritations into something different, we will be more willing to do it again in the future. Hopefully we'll start *thinking green*—reduce and recycle—instead of seeing red.

My friend Kathy told me how she lost a gold crown on her tooth. She wasn't concerned about finding it until her dentist told her it was worth $1000. So Kathy searched and searched until she found it. Recycling became very important because of what it would cost to replace it.

When I was a little girl and angrily slammed the door and trapped my grandmother on the balcony, I didn't understand that anger is a powerful human emotion that needs to be controlled. I've since learned that getting angry doesn't make me a bad person. And I've discovered that the real issue isn't whether I get angry but *what I do with that anger.* Do I express it in a selfish, harmful way? Or do I accept it and find constructive ways of handling it? Today I strive to do the latter. After all, why waste all that valuable energy?

TIME TO TAKE OUT THE TRASH

"Reduce" and "recycle" are two good words to remember when it comes to anger. This powerful emotion is God-given. And just as God gets angry but does not sin (Exodus 34:6), we want to accept our anger and control it rather than unleashing it on others.

1. What role does anger play in your life? Describe how it is a help or a hindrance.

2. Check the destructive styles of anger you've used in the past when responding to difficult situations. Write down the last time you responded that way and why.

   ☐ aggressive action:

   ☐ critical words:

   ☐ vengeful behavior:

   ☐ sarcastic remarks:

   ☐ withdrawing communication:

   ☐ withholding something:

3. List two things you will do this week to help reduce and recycle your frustrations and fury. For example, you might want to memorize one of the Scripture verses in this chapter, take a brisk walk, clean out a closet, or work out.

6

Who Do You
Need to Forgive?

During World War II, Corrie ten Boom and her sister, Betsie, were sent to Ravensbrück, a concentration camp in Germany. They were arrested because they hid Jews in their home in Holland who had been targeted for death by the Nazis. Betsie died in the camp. Years later Corrie wrote about Holocaust survivors, "Those who were able to *forgive* their former enemies were able also to return to the outside world and rebuild their lives, no matter what the physical scars. Those who nursed their bitterness remained invalids. It was as simple and as horrible as that."[1]

Corrie captured the healing power of forgiveness. As Christians we've been called to forgive, yet we often cling tightly to our hurts, grudges, and memories of offenses. Forgiveness isn't easy. Many of us aren't even clear about what forgiveness means. Some of us don't know how to forgive, while others simply don't want to forgive. To make matters more complicated, there are plenty of erroneous beliefs about forgiveness. One thing is clear though: unforgiveness equals trash. If neglected for any period of time, the unforgiveness garbage accumulates and becomes disgusting and toxic.

The Cost of Holding On to Resentments

Have you ever neglected to take out the garbage on collection day? Perhaps you forgot, maybe you were too tired, or possibly you were out of town. First, an unpleasant odor that gradually builds into an awful stench reminds you that the garbage wasn't taken out. Then unwanted creatures, such as gnats, flies, and maggots, appear. By not properly disposing of waste we've spawned a repulsive, unhealthy mess.

Regan and Matt ordered an extra garbage collection for the day after they were to host their daughter's rehearsal dinner. But for some reason the garbage didn't get taken away. A couple days later Matt hauled the cans behind their shed until the regular collection day came around. The night before trash day, Matt carried the cans to the curb for pickup. Only when he got back into the light did he notice maggots crawling all over his sleeves and hands. Had their garbage been disposed of in a timely way, it would not have become infested—and he would have been spared a creepy experience.

When our unresolved anger and grudges are not dealt with properly they fester, creating the emotional equivalent of maggots crawling all over us. As we discuss the meaning of forgiveness and the challenges of choosing to forgive, we'll also look at the importance of disposing long-held resentment in a timely fashion to avoid toxicity.

The Meaning of Forgiveness

Forgiveness is a *choice* or *decision* we make and the emotional process we move through as we let go of hurts and offenses that range from one-time petty grudges to repeated horrific offenses. To forgive means to "let go of what was done to us or should have been done for us and give up our rights for revenge or retaliation." The greater the hurt or injury we've experienced, the longer the process of forgiveness may take.

First it's important to define what "forgiveness" is not:

- Forgiveness *does not* mean we believe what happened was okay.

- Forgiveness *does not* mean we forget the offense.

- Forgiveness *does not* excuse someone's poor behavior.

Forgiveness may look different for everyone, depending on what's important to the person and how he or she was wronged. For instance, forgiveness for you might mean giving up your "right" to an apology, to be paid back, or to expect special treatment. For Cheryl, the fundraiser who lost her job, it meant giving up her "right" to be treated fairly in the workplace so she could move on without bitterness.

Jesus is our best example of how forgiveness can be lived out in the midst of the most devastating of situations. When he was nailed to the cross, he forgave his enemies. He gave up his right to be treated with respect and his rights to earthly glory and majesty. He might not have *felt* like forgiving, but he made the *decision* to do so. Regarding his executioners he said, "Father, forgive them, for they do not know what they are doing" (Luke 23:34).

Forgiveness is difficult. By focusing on the choices we *can make* as we confront the challenges that come with forgiving, we'll have an easier time.

TRASH TALK

Forgiving the unforgivable is hard. So was the cross: hard words, hard wood, hard nails.

WILLIAM S. STODDARD

The Benefits of Forgiveness

Researchers have found forgiveness dramatically improves the quality of our lives physically and emotionally, which in turn positively impacts our relationships.

Physical Benefits

Anger we haven't dealt with is called "unresolved anger." This anger can manifest as headaches, insomnia, high blood pressure, heart palpitations, fatigue, and depression. On the other hand, forgiveness frees up our mental and physical resources, enabling us to think more clearly, have an increased level of energy, and be healthier. According to ForgivenessandHealth.com, one study of more than 2000 men found that those who diffused their anger cut their risk of stroke in half compared to men who stayed angry.

Professor Kathleen Lawler of the University of Tennessee studied the physical effects of forgiveness in adults, ages 28 to 70. First, subjects filled out questionnaires about their mental and physical health. She then measured their blood pressure, heart rate, and forehead muscle tension before and during a session in which they told her about a time when they felt betrayed. As they told their stories, every person's blood pressure, heart rate, and muscle tension increased. But the rates of increase for those who had not forgiven their offenders were 25 percent higher than those who had forgiven. People who had not forgiven also reported going to the doctor more often for colds, infections, fatigue, and headaches. "The non-forgivers also took 25 percent more medications than those who had forgiven."[2]

Emotional and Spiritual Benefits

Penny, a woman who has faithfully prayed for me over the years, always reminds me to forgive so I'm not outsmarted by Satan. The evil one is happy when we hold on to unforgiveness because of the division, conflict, and turmoil it creates. The apostle Paul told us to forgive "in order that Satan might not outwit us. For we are not unaware of his schemes" (2 Corinthians 2:11). He also said, "'In your anger do not sin'…and do not give the devil a foothold" (Ephesians 4:26-27). Instead of giving the devil an opportunity to cause more problems, we want to focus on the healing and love that comes through forgiveness.

In 2005, there was a horrific school shooting in an Amish community. Charles Roberts killed five young girls and severely wounded five other girls at their schoolhouse one fall morning before killing himself. In a testament to the life-giving power of forgiveness, the

Amish families refused to hold any grudges or seek any type of retribution. The local secular community and even the nation as a whole was astounded when the Amish set up a fund for the murderer's wife and children. Jonas Beiler wrote, "[The Amish] have learned that blame and vengeance are toxic, while forgiveness and reconciliation disarm their grief. Even in the valley of the shadow of death they know how to live well."[3]

Imagine how their forgiveness impacted the family of the murderer. I can't help but think that the response of the Amish enabled the killer's wife and children to better handle any guilt, sadness, and shame they may have experienced. By refusing to blame, torment, or condemn this family, the Amish didn't allow Satan to wreak even more destruction in their Lancaster County community. Forgiveness enabled the Amish to cope with their personal losses and allowed them to be a tremendous blessing to the perpetrator's innocent family.

Relationship Benefits

Unforgiveness is not attractive. In contrast to the Christlike response of the Amish, think about a time when you had to deal with a coldhearted person who refused to let go of a long-held hurt. Now consider what unforgiveness may be doing to you. It's painful to see unforgiveness in ourselves, but as one man said to me, "It's only in looking back that I realize how much all my relationships were poisoned because of the bitterness I held toward my ex-wife."

The Challenges and Choices of Forgiveness

Even when we understand the benefits that come with forgiveness, that doesn't mean we don't struggle with making the decision to do so. Here are some of the challenges I often hear followed by the healthy choices we can make in response to them.

The Challenge: Why must I forgive? They don't deserve my forgiveness. They never said, "I'm sorry."

You don't have to forgive. But if you want to obey God, Scripture is quite clear on the issue. In the sixth chapter of Matthew, Jesus says that when we forgive others, we will be forgiven. Then he said, "But if you do not forgive men their sins, your Father will not forgive your sins" (verse 15). What possible good can come to us if we knowingly disobey God? Just like a child who willfully defies a parent, our lack of forgiveness comes with consequences, the most critical of which is that we won't be forgiven by God for our offenses.

And if we want the kind of power behind our prayers that can move mountains, Jesus tells us that if we hold *anything against anyone* we need to forgive:

> I tell you the truth, if anyone says to this mountain, "Go, throw yourself into the sea," and does not doubt in his heart but believes that what he says will happen, it will be done for him. Therefore I tell you, whatever you ask for in prayer, believe that you have received it, and it will be yours. And when you stand praying, if you hold anything against anyone, forgive him, so that your Father in heaven may forgive you your sins (Mark 11:23-25).

Author Catherine Marshall talked about her struggle with forgiveness. When she realized that Jesus talks about forgiveness right after mentioning mountain-moving faith, she determined that she would not hold "anything against anyone" that would limit the power of her prayers. At the advice of a friend, Catherine started to journal. Writing helped her let go of the grudges and little things as well as the major offenses she'd held against people in her life.[4]

After reading Catherine's story, I recognized that I often overlook the importance of dealing with petty irritations that pop up in daily living. My natural tendency is to discount these little resentments until I have a trash bag full of them. In my mind I decided they were no big deal. In fact, I've heard people suggest forgiveness is needed only for deep wounds, major injustices, and horrific abuses. But the truth is that "anything against anyone" means *every* offense, large or small, against any person.

After hearing me teach at a conference, one woman wrote, "I decided to use my journal as a dumping ground where I could let go and release. I'm purposing to check my heart to see areas where I might be struggling in releasing *someone from something.* I'm bringing that to God, offering that to him [letting it go], and waiting for his work to continue in that room of my house—the bitterness room."

Your Choice: I don't feel like forgiving, and it doesn't seem fair to forgive. But I choose to forgive the little grudges and the big offenses because I want to be forgiven *and have healthy relationships.*

The Challenge: Why should I bother to forgive? They'll just do it again anyway.

A single mother once asked me why she should forgive after hearing me speak at her church. She said, "My ex-husband repeatedly exposes our 14-year-old daughter to sexually lewd situations. I've asked him to stop but he refuses. I've tried to get legal assistance to help protect my daughter but so far it's failed."

Given that her ex-husband shows no remorse or desire to change his actions, he will probably continue his current behavior. Unless she gets legal muscle on her side, she's right to assume that she will be forgiving him repeatedly. So why should she bother?

First, Jesus never put a limit on the number of times we should forgive. He never said, "Forgive someone 50 times and that's it." The apostle Peter asked if forgiving seven times was good enough, and Jesus replied, "Seven! Hardly. Try seventy times seven" (Matthew 18:22 MSG). I don't know about you, but unless I'm keeping a detailed record of how many times I've forgiven someone, I'm going to lose count somewhere after 20—which is Jesus' point. We need to forgive a countless number of times if necessary.

We are not in control of other people's poor behavior choices.

Forgiving or not forgiving a person *does nothing to change their actions.* Sometimes we *think* that if we don't forgive we exert some sort of power over the offender. But that's not true. And when we choose not to forgive, we hurt ourselves emotionally and physically.

My reply to the single mother who asked me why she should bother to forgive was, "Forgiveness most likely won't change your ex-husband. But forgiveness will change you. It will enable you to grieve the loss of your daughter's innocence. It will help you to heal, and it will protect your health and your relationships from the toxic poison of bitterness. It will help you redirect the strength of your emotions into a positive direction to deal with the problem."

Your Choice: I can't control someone else's behavior by forgiving them. But I can choose to forgive and protect myself and my relationships from the harmful effects of long-held resentments.

The Challenge: I know I need to forgive, but right now I want to be angry.
Christie recently broke up with her fiancé, and she had lots to be angry about. For starters, her fiancé and someone Christie thought was a dear friend had been sexually involved for months.

TRASH TALK

Ongoing forgiveness keeps toxic, deadly emotions from building up. Daily forgiveness is my foremost prescription for a person's total mental, emotional, spiritual, and physical health.

DON COLBERT, MD

Anger is a common emotion that keeps reappearing during a time of loss and grief, especially after the initial shock and numbness are gone. As long as Christie is grieving, she is wise to address those feelings. Short-term, being angry is a healthy response. The longer she holds on to fury though, the harder it will be to forgive and let go. Anger and hostility can take root in our hearts and grow quickly into bitterness. Christie could find herself more "at home" with her anger than with the positive feelings of peace and joy that forgiveness can bring. The notion that it will be easier to forgive later is simply false.

Barbara lost her young son in a fire. She held on to her rage for more than 20 years. She was furious with the insurance company because of all the battles she fought with them. She was irate with friends whom she described as clueless about what she was going through. As long as she was consumed with rage, Barbara felt powerful and in control. She believed her fury was punishing people for their insensitivity. But in fact the anger was hurting her. She became a negative, complaining person people avoided as much as possible.

Tyler Perry, writer and producer of many movies including *The Diary of an Angry Black Woman*, learned how much better life could be when he gave up his rage. Tyler had an extremely abusive childhood. He was often beaten by his father who didn't appreciate his son's artistic gift of writing.

Years later Tyler ran into financial problems and forged his father's signature on a car loan. When the car was repossessed and his father found out about the default and its impact on his credit, he called Tyler and unloaded his fury. During this heated conversation Tyler finally expressed all the rage he'd held on to for years. When he was done, and after a long pause, Tyler heard his father say for the first time, "I love you."

Tyler said, "After we hung up, I felt light, empty, and exhausted. I knew that I would never again look at my father in hurt or anger. But in a strange way, I also sensed that something had died. I sat crying for hours, as if I were in mourning. My energy source, my fight, the rage that had moved me every day—it was all gone. Slowly but surely, I began to fuel my days with joy instead of fury. That year— call it coincidence—my play sold out."[5]

Like Tyler's experience, when we let go of the bitterness and anger that once motivated us to get up each day, we too might feel a strange emptiness. However, we now have more room for love and joy and the energy to make a positive impact in the lives of others.

Your Choice: I will forgive, but short-term I need to grieve. I will find ways to express my anger constructively before it becomes a permanent part of me.

The Challenge: I've honestly tried to let go and forgive, but as soon as I see the person I get upset again and all the bitterness returns.

We often expect forgiveness to be easy or instantaneous. It's not. We get discouraged when we realize we're still holding on to something. We start to believe we need more faith or we simply don't have what it takes to forgive.

Forgiveness is a process, not a once-and-done deal. It usually includes lots of little forgivenesses along the way. It's normal to have painful, negative feelings pop up toward those who've hurt you—especially when you still have to interact with them regularly. For example, every time Zack's ex-wife came to pick up the children and looked at him with a belittling smirk, he felt bitter again about how she had manipulated and deceived him during their marriage. "At those times," he said, "I have to remind myself that here's an opportunity to let go of another piece of bitterness."

When you come face-to-face with someone who caused you harm, ask God for the strength to do what is right. I love what legendary football coach Tom Landry said: "Setting a goal is not the main thing. It is deciding how you will go about achieving it and *staying with the pain.*"

If your goal is to forgive then, like Zack, you may go through some excruciatingly painful moments when you don't *feel* like letting go. Despite those feelings, choose to stay in the process. Remember: Forgiveness *is not* a feeling.

Your Choice: I can't let go as quickly as I would like. The wounds are still deep. But I will choose forgiveness now and continue choosing to forgive for my emotional health.

The Challenge: *Someone once told me if I've truly forgiven then I'll forget what happened.*

This is a common myth. We don't have to forget to forgive. I like what Dr. David Stoop advocates about the belief that we should forgive and forget. He says that not only do we *not* forget, but remembering what occurred protects us from the same thing happening again. He writes about one woman who was sexually abused by her father when she was eight years old. She tried hard to forget and pretend it never happened. Unfortunately, years later, this same woman came back to Dr. Stoop for counseling. This time she was distraught because *her* daughter, now eight years old, had been molested by the same man.[6]

What if instead of trying to forget what her father had done, ignoring her memories, and overlooking the fact there was no remorse or change in him, she had forgiven him but determined to be more cautious around him?

Remembering what happened helps us decide to learn new, protective ways of responding to those who don't deserve our trust. Suppose a friend of yours is continually criticizing and demeaning you. Do you want to set yourself up for constant abuse by forgetting her pattern of hurtfulness? Remembering what happens when you spend time with her can help you distance yourself and limit future interactions.

Caution: to remember an offense is one thing; to dwell on it is something different. Dwelling on an event keeps you stuck in unforgiveness.

Your Choice: I will forgive, but I choose to learn when it is wise to protect and distance myself.

The Challenge: I can forgive others, but I have problems forgiving myself.

Although God is the only person who can forgive, as Christians we sometimes find it difficult to receive his unconditional forgiveness that is ours when we ask him. We don't feel like we deserve such kindness. And we often feel better if we punish ourselves in some way. It somehow eases our conscience to berate ourselves and try to make us pay for what we did.

One woman I met had numerous affairs, one of which ended her marriage. Over the years since her divorce, she has sabotaged one loving relationship after another. This is her way of paying herself back for the harm she caused her ex-husband and family 20 years or so ago.

In our own broken ways we try to be little gods, tormenting ourselves for the stupid or awful things we've done. Accepting the good and bad in ourselves isn't easy, but it's essential if we are going to heal and be free to move on. So let go and give Jesus your pain and disappointment. Don't be weighed down by condemnation, and don't accept any voices in your head that continually remind you of your wrongs. Remember the truth of Romans 8:1: "There is now no condemnation for those who are in Christ Jesus."

Years ago I said something hurtful to a friend. I couldn't seem to let myself off the hook for my thoughtless comment. One afternoon I apologized once more. I'll never forget how light I felt when he said in the kindest, most loving way, "Don't worry about it, Georgia. I'm willing to carry your baggage."

This image has stuck with me because that's what God says to each one of us when we can't seem to forgive ourselves for our poor choices and mistakes. He says, "Let me lighten your burdens. Let me carry your load. Just give it to me and know you're forgiven."

Your Choice: I will confess what I have done and surrender my disappointment in myself. I will accept God's grace and mercy.

The Challenge: I'm mad at God. I can't forgive him for what he allowed to happen.

Emily had a husband and three daughters, but she was lonely and angry because, as she said, "God took both my parents away within a two-and-a-half-month period." Although she believed her mom and dad were both with God, that didn't ease her pain. "My anger continued to harden my heart, and I took my frustrations out on everyone around me," she shared.

This continued for two years.

"Finally I knew it was time to let go of all the anguish and concentrate on living and loving those around me," Emily said. "It was time to love and trust God again."

Unlike the people around us, God is more than able to handle the brunt of our honest anger until we grieve and can accept what he has brought into or taken out of our lives.

Your Choice: I will pour out my hurt and anger to God, and then I will let those emotions go so I can love and trust him completely once more.

Right now would be a good time for you to explore your situation:

- Is there anyone you need to forgive? Has someone treated you unjustly? Has anyone been insensitive to your feelings? Has someone tried to destroy you emotionally, financially, or physically?

- Are there issues you've been holding on to for years that you need to let go of?

- Will you choose to forgive?

Signs That It's Time to Forgive

Stella was conned out of two million dollars by her husband (now her ex-husband). Despite the hard evidence, he continues to deny any wrongdoing. She told me, "I'm having problems focusing at work. I'm short with my employees. I suffer from one sinus infection after another. To this day some of my stepchildren won't talk to me. All I can think of is how I want him to hurt like he hurt me."

Set on revenge, Stella called her ex-husband's employer to report "what a lying cheat they had working for them." She emailed his co-workers, attempting to stir up problems with his relationships. She lost sleep coming up with other ways to hurt him. Eventually Stella's friends started to avoid her. When a few of her co-workers hinted that she "had a chip on her shoulder," Stella ignored their comments and continued plotting.

There is no doubt Stella was betrayed by her husband and deeply hurt by his actions. She *is not* wrong to be upset. What happened was awful, and what's worse, her ex-husband seems to have no remorse. But instead of acting on her natural inclination to retaliate, Stella needs to recognize that while she's trying to destroy her ex-husband's life, she's destroying her own. Her bitterness is damaging her health and her relationships. I agree with author and theologian Lewis Smedes who said that forgiveness "is the only remedy of pain you didn't have coming and pain you can't get rid of."

If you're dwelling on what someone did to you, *choose forgiveness*. If you're wallowing in self-pity, *choose to work through your hurting feelings* rather than doing something wrong.

One of my friends owned a recycling business several years ago. "At first we recycled rags along with paper, plastic, cardboard, and aluminum cans," she told me one afternoon. "However, we stopped collecting rags because they attracted the rats."

"Why did rats like the rags?" I asked.

"They kept them warm in the winter and provided great nesting material."

Unforgiveness is like collecting rags. The cost and consequences of bitterness far outweigh anything we might gain. To be emotionally whole, choose to discard your resentments in a timely fashion. Don't put it off. You don't want to attract the emotional equivalent of an infestation of rats, maggots, and other undesirables.

TIME TO TAKE OUT THE TRASH

I've heard it said that "forgiveness is a gift you give to yourself by giving something away." Even if the other person doesn't know it or deserve it, you will be free because you gave your trash away.

1. If you haven't yet made the choice to forgive someone, why not?

   ☐ Are you waiting for an apology, an explanation, or a gesture of making amends?

   ☐ Are you waiting for the people who have offended or hurt you to admit they have a problem or to change their behavior?

   ☐ Are you punishing the people who hurt you?

   ☐ Are you still grieving the pain and sorrow?

   ☐ Do you think forgiveness is a sign of weakness?

   ☐ Other (please explain):

2. What can you do today to help you forgive in the situations you considered when answering question 1?

3. Do you have a tendency to dwell on past hurts and pain?

4. Are there signals alerting you to the fact you need to forgive—and do it soon?

- ☐ Are you consumed with thoughts of revenge?
- ☐ Are friends or family keeping their distance?
- ☐ Are you stuck in a cycle of negative thinking and self-pity?
- ☐ Are your resentments affecting your health and ability to focus?

5. Whose name do you need to put into the following prayer? Why not do it now?

> Lord, I am ready to forgive *[person's name]* and lay down my desire for vengeance. I don't know how to be totally free of all the pain and bitterness, but I'm willing to give it to you and learn from you. Right now I'm choosing to forgive because I want to be forgiven by you and be free to live life to the fullest in you. Thank you. Amen.

7

Are You Stuck in the Forgiveness Process?

I made the choice to forgive, but how do I get rid of all this rage and bitterness?" This woman's concern echoes the thoughts of many who are trapped in long-held resentments. She discovered that making the choice to forgive is one thing; working her way through all the related emotions is another.

Just as we have waste cans in our kitchens and garbage bins in our garage, we also have electronic trash on our computers. If I want to completely delete a file on my computer, there are several steps I need to take. First, I highlight the name of the file in my list of documents, and then I hit the delete key. After I confirm that I want to delete the file, it appears to be deleted. It's not gone, however. I can retrieve it by clicking on my computer's recycle bin icon, highlighting the name of the file, and selecting "restore." Then the "deleted" file is returned to its original location.

To completely remove the file after it's in my recycle bin, I have to highlight the file, choose "delete," and then confirm my choice. Clicking "yes" means it is gone for most practical purposes. (Tech gurus will still be able to find it on my hard drive.) Forgiveness is like deleting a file. Making the choice to forgive is the beginning of the process. It's a first step, but there's more work to be done. To completely rid yourself of potentially toxic emotions, you need to work through your feelings until you are emotionally healed.

As my author and counselor friend Leslie Vernick, writes, "I find people either forgive too quickly before they have done the emotional work or forget and bury the hurt and anger." Both of those approaches, skimming over the process or burying the pain, will keep you stuck in your junk and trapped in your trash. Since your goal is to forgive and be healed, it's important to complete the emotional work.

Forgiveness Is a Process

Even after choosing to forgive, it's normal to have times of discouragement, to wonder, "Is there an end to my anger?" In spite of your feelings, you can find freedom from grudges and bitterness by being *intentional* about forgiving. When working through the process of forgiveness, it's important to:

- verbalize how you feel
- remember what God has done for you
- recognize forgiveness takes time and effort
- ask yourself searching questions to evaluate where you are
- watch for signs you are progressing
- commemorate the act of forgiveness

Let's start this process by taking the first step.

Verbalize How You Feel

Telling your story, including expressing and naming your feelings, is one of the ways you heal. Talking or writing about what you experienced, rather than silently stewing in your bitterness, is therapeutic.

I used to discount how important this step is in the forgiveness process. When a friend did something that violated my trust, I told myself, *Georgia, you've written about forgiveness. You need to forgive her.* And that was true. I did need to let it go. But instead I glossed

over what happened. And that felt like I was saying it wasn't important. I wasn't validating the part of me that was hurt. When I allowed
myself to voice how I'd been wounded ("She violated my trust. She
knew that was important to me."), then it was easier to move on.

Sometimes giving a voice to our hurts means communicating in
an open way directly to the person involved: "That really offended
me" or "I didn't appreciate how you dumped on me." At other times,
and for various reasons, it's not possible or safe to communicate in
person. In those instances, you can verbalize your feelings through
prayer, writing, drawing, or talking with someone safe. Teri jokingly
said something unkind to her pastor. Later he approached her and
said, "What you said hurt me very much…But I want you to know
I forgive you, and it's forgotten."

Teri was mortified.

However, her pastor's interactions with her over the next couple
of months showed he didn't hold her thoughtless comment against
her. He hadn't gone to others and shared how she'd wounded him.
He'd said what he wanted to say to her that day and moved on.

Teri said, "I later thanked him for modeling God's forgiveness.
He got tears in his eyes when I told him how his recent interactions
with me proved he really had let it go."

Giving voice to our hurt and giving grace to the other person
prevents bitterness from taking hold. As the apostle Paul said, "See
to it that no one misses the grace of God and that no bitter root
grows up to cause trouble and defile many" (Hebrews 12:15).

Remember What God Has Done for You

The next step is critical because after you've verbalized how you
feel, it's easy to get stuck there. People can get into the habit of
rehearsing the ways they've been hurt and wounded. Repeatedly
dwelling on what they've suffered only adds to their misery, hinders
their healing, and harms others.

A spirit of gratitude is a great antidote to resentment. When
you're tempted to slip into the mindset of retaliation, remind yourself of what God has done for you. Remember how his grace and

mercy have erased a multitude of sins you've committed. Then follow his example with the person you are dealing with.

The place where Jesus died was a garbage dump for
the whole city. He died for all the garbage in our souls.
LIVING WORD COMMUNITY CHURCH

Psychologist David Stoop writes,

> We need to be careful that we do not take forgiveness out
> of its spiritual context, because forgiveness can best be
> understood only in the context of our being forgiven by
> God. The theological and spiritual roots of forgiveness are
> what give it its healing power. Apart from that, forgiveness
> can be a helpful tool but never to the same degree as when
> it is connected to the reality of God's forgiveness of us.[1]

Jesus tells the story of a servant who begged for forgiveness from
a king. This servant owed the king a lot of money but didn't have the
funds to repay his loan. The servant pleaded for more time. The king
took pity on this servant and generously canceled the entire debt.

Then the servant, now debt-free, turned around and demanded
immediate payment of a loan he'd made to one of his fellow servants.
This person was unable to repay his loan and begged for more time.
The first servant refused his fellow servant's request and had the man
thrown into debtor's prison. And what did the king say when he
heard about the unforgiveness of the first servant?

> "You wicked servant," he said, "I canceled all that debt
> of yours because you begged me to. Shouldn't you have
> had mercy on your fellow servant just as I had on you?"
> In anger his master turned him over to the jailers to be
> tortured, until he should pay back all he owed (Matthew 18:32-34).

Although the first servant had been treated with kindness and generosity by the king, he lost sight of this gift. Instead of experiencing the healing power that comes from being forgiven and results in passing on that forgiveness to another, this servant ended up being tortured in prison.

In the same way, when we focus only on what has been done *to* us and how *we've been hurt,* we put ourselves in an emotional and spiritual prison. Realizing how we've sinned against God and yet how gracious and loving he is toward us should change our perspective and free us to experience his healing power and share his mercy with others. As Lewis Smedes writes, "When we forgive, we set a prisoner free and then discover that the prisoner we set free was us."[2]

Never forget how much it cost God to forgive you for your sins and shortcomings. He gave up his one and only Son so that you could be forgiven. Oswald Chambers says, "Forgiveness is the divine miracle of grace. The cost to God was the Cross of Christ."[3]

Recognize Forgiveness Takes Time and Effort

During the question-and-answer period at a recent conference, one woman asked, "Isn't there any way to speed up this process of forgiveness? I'm trying to forgive my ex, but it's taking way too long. Do you have any tips? I want to get this behind me and move on."

This is a common question. We prefer quick solutions—the quick fixes. We don't like discomfort and pain. The problem with seeking a fast approach is that it ignores the depth of healing needed when we've been wounded. It ignores the struggles we face when we've been violated in some way. We can't speed up the process, but we can be *intentional* about taking the time and doing the work necessary for healing.

Trying to rush through the process is like quickly opening a bottle of shaken-up carbonated beverage. Liquid spews all over and creates a big mess. The only way to safely relieve the built-up pressure is to do it carefully, a little bit at a time. Likewise, we continue releasing our hurts and pain a little at a time until the emotional fizz, if you will, has subsided.

Jordon learned firsthand what a slow effort the forgiveness process can be when she had to work through her bottled-up emotions after being sexually abused by a close friend of her family. It took 25 years for her to decide to finally deal with her long-held bitterness. The anger, hatred, and distrust she felt about her abuser had spilled over into her other relationships with men. In fact, the only man she wasn't angry at was her dad, who had treated her with kindness and respect.

To learn how to forgive, Jordon sought the help of an excellent Christian counselor. She joined a spiritual group at her church called "Restoring Eve." She asked people to pray for her as she worked through her unresolved anger and grieved the loss of her innocence. Jordon was doing all the right things, yet she said, "I couldn't seem to move past this. It felt like something kept me trapped. I kept wondering, *Why did he do it? Was it my fault because I used to sit on his lap as he read to me?*

At a fall women's retreat I attended, Jordon showed me a picture she crayoned symbolizing the burden she carried. The background was filled with lovely shades of blue and green with a little red. What caught my attention was the image she drew of herself and the burden she carried. She held a stiff, dark, almost evil-looking body.

Getting rid of this dead weight was her challenge. Over the next year, I watched as she continued to pray, journal, and talk about her ongoing struggles. "I've already chosen to forgive him, but why can't I let it go? Sometimes I wonder if I'll ever be free of this burden," she said.

Despite her doubts, one day it came together for her. When I saw Jordon at a weekend retreat, she was filled with excitement. "Georgia," she said, "I'm free! I'm truly free."

"What happened?" I asked. "Did you bury that dead body?"

"No, it's simply gone. God took it away," she said. "My therapist had me write letters from 'little Jordon' to 'big Jordon' and then the reverse. I think it was writing those letters, reading them aloud to her, and then talking about them that finally put all the pieces together and gave me freedom. I wrote about what I felt and why I felt the way I did."

Jordon has given me permission to share parts of her letters with you. Writing them gave voice to the hurt and pain trapped inside her and helped her work through her anger and bitterness.

> Dear Big Jordon,
>
> I feel really bad about what just happened. Why did he touch me like that? Did I do something to encourage it? I remember sitting on his lap (like I always did). We were playing. He was tickling me. We had our evening ice cream, and we were sitting there watching TV. I remember I was too young to wear a bra, but I had just started getting boobs. He was scratching my back. His hands were rough but it felt nice. Then he reached his hand around to the front and cupped my boobs and just held them. I made myself stiff and slowly got off his lap and went into my room.
>
> I remember locking the door—I was afraid he might come in. I didn't know what to do. I didn't even think about telling anyone. I might have thought it was an accident...he didn't mean anything by it. It was a slip—he wouldn't have done that on purpose...I think I really tried hard to forget it ever happened—but it did happen.
>
> I'm mad about it—I'm very angry. Why would he do such a thing? I'm like a granddaughter to him. I love him. I thought he loved me. Why would he throw our relationship away like that? Why would he think it would be OK for him to touch me like that? What do I do now? I can't tell anyone. They won't believe me...
>
> Big Jordon, take this away from me and you carry it. It is too much for me to handle. I will trust you to take it and hand it over to God. Let God punish him. I'm going to let it go and forgive him. I'm never going to know why he did it and that's OK. I need to forgive myself for not

being able to handle this on my own. I forgive myself, and I love me!!

Love,
Little Jordon

Dear Little Jordon,

I am so sorry that you have to go through this. It isn't fair. It isn't right; it's not your fault at all. You are a child, and he is an adult. You have been taken advantage of. I know you feel as though you should not tell anyone... I am here to listen to you, to comfort you. Please let me take this burden from you so you do not have to carry it around. It will make your heart cold and hard. I want you to still be the wonderful girl you were meant to be. I want to take this burden away from you. Please release it. Let God punish him. You don't have to do that. Let go of what has happened to you. Know that God loves you, I love you, and your mother and father love you. Tell me everything, and we will give it over to God...You are such a light to people, and you will shine again. You can shine like a star.

I love you,
Big Jordon

Today Jordon's eyes remain bright and her countenance positive and light. She no longer hangs on to what happened. She looks forward with hope and excitement. Guess what image now represents the light, airy feeling Jordon has? It's a photograph she cut from a magazine of a group of Monarch butterflies fluttering against a brilliant blue sky.

Ask Yourself Searching Questions to Evaluate Where You Are

There can be many reasons why you might struggle with the process of forgiveness and get stuck. Asking some searching questions can get you out of your rut and move you forward. Here are a few suggestions that may help you gain awareness of what is holding you back.

Is there anything I'm afraid to do?

When Jade asked this question, she realized she feared having to tell her ex that she'd forgiven him. She didn't know that she could forgive someone without communicating that directly to the person. Because of his violent history and hearing reports that he had not changed, Jade didn't feel safe speaking to him. With the help of her counselor, she was relieved to learn she could forgive her ex and protect herself from possible further injury by not contacting him.

Each situation is different. Sometimes God does ask us to tell people we have forgiven them. Through prayer and godly counsel God will guide you as to whether you need speak to the person or simply forgive him or her in your heart.

Is there anything I'm afraid I'll have to give up?

Are you concerned that completely forgiving will make you look like a doormat? Are you worried forgiveness will mean someone will take advantage of you or you'll lose control? Brandon was concerned that forgiveness meant he would lose control. What he discovered, however, was that once he worked through the anger of growing up with an abusive mother, he *gained more control* over his emotions. Brandon found that every little criticism, sarcastic remark, and hostile outburst from his mother no longer set him off.

Jon thought forgiving would make him look like a wimp. The idea of letting go of his right to get even seemed like something a coward would do.

I recommend you talk to people who have endured much and forgiven much. You'll soon realize forgiveness takes courage and strength. To quote Gandhi, a political and spiritual leader in India, "The weak can never forgive. Forgiveness is the attribute of the strong."

Am I willing to let go of the energy from my negative emotions?

Whether we want to admit it or not, there are some payoffs to staying angry or bitter. Strong negative emotions can make us feel powerful and energetic. Author and surgeon Clark Gerhart says that physiological factors affect how we respond to our emotions.

He notes that some of our negative responses, such as unforgive-ness, make us feel good because they excite our internal reward sys-tem.[4] If you have ever been hurt and later felt good holding on to the grudges, you've experienced an "excited internal reward system."

To really forgive, you need to be willing to experience the short-term letdown that comes when you release negative emotions. For example, a friend betrayed some information I confided to her. She didn't realize I knew what she'd done because a mutual friend told me about the disclosure. From that point on I wanted to let this per-son know in some subtle way that she'd been caught. I'd been hurt, and the thought of hurting her back felt good and right.

One morning, during my devotion time, I realized I had to stop looking for the chance to get even. Letting go of my grudge was a real letdown. It amazed me how much I had been anticipating the look on her face when she found out what I knew. But once again God reminded me that forgiveness is not a feeling; it is a decision I choose to make.

Have I grieved what I lost?

Grieving is part of the forgiveness process. We usually think about working through unresolved anger when we forgive, but it's equally important to address the related sadness and loss. If I were sexually abused as a child, I would need to grieve the loss of my innocence and the loss of my childhood. If my marriage ended in divorce, I may need to grieve the loss of my lifestyle, my home, my financial reserves, and an "onsite" father for my children.

Reece's son was an alcoholic. One night he took her car and demol-ished it. Several months later, as Reece processed her hurt and anger, she said to her counselor, "I know I've forgiven him now because I'm not angry anymore. I'm just sad." What Reece didn't understand was that the process of forgiveness *includes* working through *all* the emo-tions surrounding the offense—including sadness.

Am I giving this incident more importance than it deserves?

More than 30 years ago Addison had an abortion. Even though

she had confessed this sin and asked God for forgiveness, she continued having problems letting go. One morning during her quiet time, she felt like God was quietly pointing out the ways she continued to berate and punish herself over this issue. She needed to give him this burden so she could be freer to focus on her family and ministry. Addison decided to do an exercise a close friend had shared with her a few days earlier. (If you need to evaluate whether an incident is taking up too much time and effort than it deserves, why not try this exercise too?) Here's an adapted version:

- On a blank sheet of paper, draw a circle in the center of page. Write one phrase describing the mistake or choice you've made.

- Now draw 12 more circles on the page. Within each circle insert a phrase describing a wise choice you've made or one of your good qualities, strengths, skills, and talents.

- Holding the paper at arm's length, what do you notice?

Do you find your mistake minimized by the many positive qualities you possess? Or is the circle in the center of the paper much larger? Does this one choice seem to swallow up all the other positive traits around it?[5]

As Addison studied her circles, she realized she'd been giving the abortion more importance than everything else in her life. The circle representing her abortion was bigger than the circle symbolizing her relationship with God. It was bigger than the circle signifying her role as a mother of two children. It was bigger than the circles representing all the wonderful ways she loved her husband and helped others.

She realized how she had worn herself out trying to do what God had already done. Instead of embracing God's love and forgiveness, Addison was trying to make up for her mistake on her own. But her attempts to make things right were never good enough, never big enough. Finally Addison chose to put this incident in its proper perspective and accept God's forgiveness. Her burden was lifted.

Addison redrew all the circles and did the exercise again. This time the circle with the word "abortion" was smaller than many of the other circles—especially the ones representing her relationship with Christ and his forgiveness. Once she could put this incident in its proper perspective and accept God's forgiveness, she could experience more of who God created her to be rather than constantly striving to make up for having chosen to get an abortion.

How about you?

- Are there any poor choices or mistakes you've magnified or blown out of proportion?

- Are you willing to change the way you look at that event?

- Will you accept God's love and forgiveness?

Are there triggers causing an emotional setback?

A "trigger" is something that can, within a split second, set off an intense emotional response. A trigger can be anything from a whiff of perfume, a song on the radio, the aroma of a special food, a fleeting image, or crossing paths with a certain person. For example, the late author Joy Jacobs was sexually abused by a family member. Years later God allowed her abuser to come back into her life. Here's how she described that traumatic time:

> I thought I had forgiven him, but I found myself experiencing floods of resentment and anger so strong that I

actually felt physically nauseated in his presence. Anxiety and contempt surged through me each time I looked at him or heard his voice. Worse yet, vivid memories of the initial abuse—memories now almost 40 years old—replayed in vivid color on the screen of my mind.[6]

Like Joy's experience, it's normal to have something suddenly remind us of particular incidents. These occurrences don't necessarily mean we're stuck in the emotions, but they usually signify there are more feelings to work through. Perhaps this is the time to work through things at a deeper emotional level.

Watch for Signs You Are Progressing

Forgiveness heals the deepest of wounds and frees us of resentment that may threaten our health and relationships. However, scars and ongoing consequences of living with what someone did to us often remain. How do we know when we've truly released our bitterness? One way we're aware we're making progress is when we see the signs of forgiveness in our lives. What are these signs?

TRASH TALK

If you are trying to forgive, even if you manage forgiving in fits and starts, if you forgive today, hate again tomorrow, and have to forgive again the day after, you are a forgiver. Most of us are amateurs, bungling duffers sometimes. So what? In this game nobody is an expert. We are all beginners.

LEWIS SMEDES

Emma had been diligently working her way toward complete forgiveness of her ex-husband, specifically involving his use of drugs and infidelity:

When he left after 20 years of marriage, I lost almost everything. I lost my home and had to live with my parents. I had to go back to school and scrimp to make ends meet. One of my children attempted suicide, and another one became addicted to drugs.

After years of counseling, I thought I had completely forgiven him. But one day someone asked me if I could wish him well. I knew my answer was no...That's when I realized I hadn't forgiven him 100 percent.

If you're wondering whether you've forgiven someone 100 percent, see if these signs are evident:

- You no longer put your life on hold. You're not waiting for an apology or for the person to change.

- You no longer need to go over and over what happened. You don't dwell on the incident or stay up at night mulling over how you've been hurt.

- You no longer want to harm or see bad things happen to this person. You are not looking for revenge or payback.

- You no longer overreact when you see or have to talk to him or her. Yes, you may tense up, but you don't react with hostility and rage.

- You accept the person for who he or she is.

- You begin to see the person's choices and actions in a new light.

- You feel more compassion toward the person.

- You pray for the person and his or her needs.

- You interact with others without carrying a chip on your shoulder.

- You've reconstructed your life and started again.

- You consistently experience God's peace, love, and joy.

Within months after Bethany's fiancé, Graham, broke their engagement, he married one of his past girlfriends. As Bethany wrestled with his deceit and her anger, she comforted herself with the idea that his marriage would never last. She fantasized about the day she would be able to say, "I told you it wouldn't work. How could it when you never dealt with your stuff?" But as Bethany worked through her feelings with help from a counselor, she no longer obsessed about someday gloating over his pain and saying, "I told you so."

Two years later, when a mutual friend told Bethany that Graham was divorced, Bethany felt nothing but compassion for him. "All I thought about was how devastated he must be," she said. "I wanted to call him and tell him how sorry I was that it didn't work out. I realized then that my bitterness and hatred toward him were gone."

The apostle Paul said,

> I pray that you, being rooted and established in love, may have power, together with all the saints, to grasp how wide and long and high and deep is the love of Christ, and to know this love that surpasses knowledge—that you may be filled to the measure of all the fullness of God (Ephesians 3:17-19).

My friend, Linda Jewell, uses an image of the incredible range of God's love to remind herself of the process of forgiveness. To her, forgiveness is like throwing something into the Grand Canyon. Using her analogy, little offenses or grudges are like pebbles that we simply toss into the canyon. The big or deeply entrenched hurts are like pushing huge boulders into the canyon.

With the boulders, we work and work pushing each one, but we don't know how much progress we're making. We can't see how close to the edge of the canyon the boulder is because it blocks our view. We pray to God to help us remove this huge thing from our lives. Then one day, as we continue to push that boulder of trashy stuff, it suddenly teeters and plunges over the edge. We no longer feel its weight because it's fallen into the grand canyon of God's love, never to be retrieved. Our work is complete, and we are free to move on.

Commemorate the Act of Forgiveness

Because the process of forgiveness is neither quick nor easy, many people find it helpful to do something symbolic to commemorate the acts of letting go and forgiving. Doing something tangible can bring closure to healing and initiate freedom. Some people write a final letter and then burn it. Others plant a tree to celebrate new life. You might choose to get rid of something given to you by the person that was once very important to you. You could light a row of candles, each one symbolizing a portion of your experience or loss. (You realize part of your life is over when the candles burn out or you blow them out.)

For more than a year Tracy had been working through the anger and pain surrounding her daughter's divorce. Her son-in-law, Brandon, refused to acknowledge his sexual addiction and seek help. When the divorce was final and there was no hope for reconciliation, Tracy knew she now had to do something with her daughter's wedding bouquet. Tracy had preserved it and planned to put it under a beautiful glass dome and give it to her daughter as a Christmas present. When her daughter's marital troubles came to light, Tracy had hidden the bouquet but hadn't given up hope for reconciliation.

During a devotion time, Tracy read about the different offerings the Israelites gave God. She learned that a tithe represented giving a portion of income or crops, whereas a drink offering was something that was totally poured out or completely given to God. Tracy decided to symbolically surrender her hopes and dreams for her daughter's marriage. As she offered praise and thanksgiving to God, she dropped the dried bridal bouquet into the trash can and felt a sense of closure.

Being able to look back and remember what you did in commemoration will also remind you of the forgiveness choice you made. When you choose to do something symbolic, you will probably experience a sense of lightness, peace, and inner joy that comes from completely forgiving. Forgiveness brings freedom and is a time for celebration!

Forgiveness Is Worth the Work

If we don't want to be bogged down with bitterness, we need to take the time and make the effort to get rid of any toxic emotions we've been harboring. We want to free up our emotional and physical resources so we have the space and energy for what's important to us. Paul said it best, "Get rid of all bitterness, rage and anger, brawling and slander, along with every form of malice. Be kind and compassionate to one another, forgiving each other, just as in Christ God forgave you" (Ephesians 4:31-32).

Forgiveness is worthwhile and of great value. Here's a letter I received from a woman working through forgiveness:

> I nearly suffered a breakdown dealing with the ongoing dishonesty and disloyalty of my husband. We sought counseling and have been reconciled, but now I realize I never forgave him…although I said I did.
>
> I started going to counseling again to help me work through my unresolved anger. The problem was that I was always too busy trying to keep up with my children and grandchildren and taking care of my husband that I never took care of my own emotions. I'm now taking the time to take out my trash. This has probably saved me from serious emotional consequences.

TIME TO TAKE OUT THE TRASH

1. Once you've chosen to forgive someone, how will you work through your emotions?

2. Do you tend to forgive too quickly? Why might this not be a good thing?

3. Do you tend to get frustrated when it feels like you aren't making headway? What can you do about it?

4. Are you obsessing over something that was done to you or something you did? Are you giving it more importance than it deserves?

   - If so, did you try the "letting go" circle exercise described in this chapter? If yes, how did it help? If not, take a few minutes and do it now. Did it help?

5. Think of someone you've recently forgiven. Have you partially or completely forgiven him or her? How can you tell?

☐ I no longer put my life on hold while waiting for an apology or for the person to change.

☐ I can pray for him or her without getting upset.

☐ I can see how God used the situation as an opportunity for me to grow.

☐ I feel a sense of lightness and freedom.

☐ Other (describe):

☐ Other (describe):

8

Which Losses Can Be Composted?

In the area I live in, the sanitation department has a "don't bag leaves" policy. What that means is the autumn leaves that decorate our fall landscape can't be put out with the weekly garbage. Instead we rake our leaves into wide piles a few feet from the road, and our township gathers them up and transports them to a municipal composting facility. We can also choose to shred our leaves with a lawn mower to use as mulch or compost the leaves ourselves. Leaves are considered a great resource.

What Is Compost?

Compost is the dark, rich, soil-like substance that is the result of the decaying of dead leaves and other organic material, such as grass clippings. Gardeners call compost "black gold" because, when mixed with soil, it adds a wealth of valuable nutrients, improves the soil's capacity to hold water, includes good microorganisms, and "returns to the soil a high proportion of the things agriculture takes out of it."[1] When compost is added to garden soil, the plantings become healthier and more vibrant than plants grown in regular soil.

Similarly, compost in our lives is the rich, fertile soil that results from the healthy process of taking care of the pain, deep hurts, or other negative emotions that result from our losses, shattered dreams, and broken hearts. If you've been in the habit of tossing them into the trash, please understand they are too valuable to dispose of that way. When handled properly, our losses slowly break down and are transformed into wonderful nutrients that promote new growth. Sorrows provide the substance for our emotional and spiritual growth, along with enabling us to gain new understanding and compassion for others who are suffering.

What can be composted emotionally? What are the different approaches to composting? How will we know when we have "black gold"?

What Can Be Composted?

When composting, I take fruit and vegetable scraps, grass clippings, fallen leaves, dead flowers and plants, and mix them with soil and water. Other than occasionally turning the pile over, I simply wait until nature does its work and the heap slowly but surely rots into a crumbly, earthlike material.

There are some things I never put on my compost pile. Meat scraps are forbidden because they invite unwanted critters, such as raccoons and other predators. I never put in weeds that have gone to seed or diseased plants because I don't want them to contaminate the "new soil" I'm helping to create.

═══ TRASH TALK ═══

Emotional trash from the past is unavoidable, but it is not all bad. In limited quantities, it can provide fertile ground for the sprouting of compassion, empathy, and understanding.

LAUREL MELLIN

Emotionally speaking, what can be composted are the painful losses that don't go away in a day, a month, or even longer. Experiences such as financial devastation, the loss of a home, the death of someone we love, and the end of a marriage can be added to the compost heap. These losses have finality about them. They are permanent endings that bring deep sadness.

The first step in emotional composting is to identify what has died in our lives so we can sort it out and put it in our compost pile. There are many kinds of death—the death of hopes and dreams, the termination of a job, the end of a special relationship. For example, Sarah's father hasn't spoken to her for years. He is still alive, but he is no longer part of her life. She's had to acknowledge the loss of her once-close relationship with her dad, realizing that for them things will never be like they used to be.

Rebecca has recognized her hopes and dreams for a child of her own are shattered. She'd always wanted to marry and have a family but because of a recent hysterectomy a part of that dream has died.

Another loss we often forget to acknowledge are the sorrows that come with the different seasons of life. The joy of having a baby brings the loss of freedom to come and go as we like. Our children start preschool and bring the loss of companionship. Our sons or daughters get married or move away, which brings unexpected and often difficult changes. Alison was thrilled her son wanted to be a missionary, but when he left home for an extended stay in South America, she was surprised she felt so empty and sad.

The single people among us experience the loss of freedom that results from finishing schooling and entering the work-every-day world. As they get older they may realize some of their dreams probably won't come to pass. If they are still single in their forties, their dreams of love and close companionship may seem like they'll never reach fruition.

We can also experience the destruction of our homes from a fire, flood, or other disaster. A close friend is diagnosed with breast cancer, and with it comes the destruction of the illusion that we're invincible. Divorce brings the death of our family or of friendships as we knew them. Our parents are growing old so we often face the added responsibilities that come with caring for them. And then there are the physical deaths of those we love. And our own aging gradually takes away many of our freedoms, including the abilities to drive, to remember clearly, to do the things we could do when we were younger.

Whatever the losses, acknowledge them and know that these belong on your compost pile. They can be recycled into *life-enriching experiences.* To evaluate what experiences and emotions you can compost, ask these questions:

- Who has left me or what have I lost that was very dear to me?

- Who or what did I care deeply about that has changed?

- What doors have been permanently closed?

- What has been destroyed?

- What changes are irreversible?

The following exercise will also help you visualize what can be turned into something of value:

1. Draw a large box to represent a compost bin on a piece of paper.

2. Fill the box with the words and brief descriptions that cover your various losses.

Remember that sometimes what seems dead may only be *dormant*. For instance, we may have a friendship that seems to have waned, but perhaps instead of being over, the friendship will bloom in another season. We can put the loss of a friendship as we knew it on our compost heap, but we might not want to compost the entire relationship. A key fact to remember about compost is that it's made up of *dead* material. Here's how God helped me clarify the difference:

One late August morning I closely examined some wrinkled, dried iris tubers a friend had given me. As I pulled another one from the dusty brown grocery bag, a fine cloud of dirt emerged. *Maybe they have been sitting around for too long to grow,* I thought.

I debated whether I wanted to take the time to plant them. Many were small with no hint of growth. Besides the only recollection I had of irises were the drab, brownish ones growing around a neighbor's farmhouse, so I wasn't very enthusiastic about the project to begin with.

However, this was the first year of my new garden, and I had lots of unused space. So in spite of my concerns, I dug the holes and tucked in the rhizomes.

Ten months later I was surprised by an abundance of showcase irises. Some were pale peach; others brilliant yellow. Several were a soft shade of lavender, but my favorites by far were the dazzling white ones with deep-purple edging.

Like those seemingly dead tubers, I've had times in my life when there were no signs of new growth. Instead I experienced a lot of killing frosts. But over the years I have learned to wait for spring. One of these times was when Kyle, my only child, left for his first semester in college.

When Kyle kissed me goodbye it was one more loss in a long string of final endings. I'd just completed a project

I'd poured myself into for years. My stepfather had suddenly died of a heart attack. And a year-long dating relationship was abruptly terminated (and not by me).

Because I'm a single parent, Kyle's departure left a vacant feeling in the house, in my heart, and in my life. The phone no longer rang incessantly. There was no one to talk to at six-thirty in the morning. There was no reason to prepare meals, and the endless parade of dishes and laundry vanished.

As the days passed, the house grew more hollow and silent. *No one needs me any longer. My life is over.* I felt like my purpose and life had been packed up and hauled away like the boxes of Kyle's possessions.

I poured out these feelings of sadness to the Lord one morning in late October while removing some dead annuals from my garden. I was working near a clump of irises when the Lord seemed to ask, "Did you think those irises would be so lovely when you planted them?"

"No."

"In spite of your lack of confidence," God seemed to say, "they not only bloomed that first year but for each year since. You're comparing your life—the endings in your life—to the annuals. Focus on the perennials."

His message clicked. The annuals, such as petunias and geraniums, had been destroyed by the killing frost and would not return next year. Although my perennials at the moment also looked dead, in a few months they would once again burst forth with new growth.

My life as Kyle's mother wasn't over—it was only the end of a season. I needed to grieve the end of Kyle's high school days and the time when he lived at home as a dependent. But I also needed to realize I was transitioning into a new season as his mother.

If I had added the iris tubers to my compost pile, they would have decayed and never bloomed. In the same way, if I assume an issue or circumstance is dead when it is merely dormant and I throw it into the compost pile, it will be a great loss.

Because each of us has experienced what seems like the end of something treasured, how can we know whether something has indeed ceased to exist or whether it's only in a season of dormancy? I've learned that when doubts rise, there is one thing we can't trust, and that's appearances.

A quick survey of the frozen winter landscape outside my window confirms this. The fields covered in snow display only a few remains of broken corn stalks. The branches of my maple tree are barren, with only a few crisp leaves clinging in spite of the howling wind. I search for any sign of life—any hint of new growth—and find none. It would be easy to conclude that the days of my flower garden are over, gone forever. However, history has taught me to wait for another season. In only a few months most of the landscape will be transformed. The grass, now brown and frozen in ice, will spring up a vibrant green. Most of my trees and perennials will blossom once more. This vegetation, dormant through the winter, will grow in a new season.

Sometimes we need only be patient and wait for the time of new growth.

Grief Transformed

While our sorrows go on the compost pile to be broken down, grieving is what God often uses to transform them into rich compost. Grieving, the painful process we move through as we face heartache, is the *catalyst* in the compost process. The strong emotions that come with losing something or someone we treasured are powerful. Most people don't know how to handle this intense emotional pain so they attempt to numb it with food, pain medication, alcohol, sex, or busyness. They don't realize that the *only way to healing and new life* is to grieve over what is gone. "Grieving means allowing yourself to feel your feelings, think your thoughts, lament your loss and protest your pain."[2]

When grieving, we experience many emotions, including anger. One of the most common feelings is sadness. This heart-wrenching anguish can wake you up in the middle of the night with a deep ache. We often feel paralyzed and that our lives are over. Sadness zaps our strength and interferes with our ability to concentrate, even on simple projects. Instead of reading our emails, we find ourselves staring at the computer screen without comprehension. It's difficult to do simple, routine chores, such as folding laundry or unloading the dishwasher. Tragic loss quickly depletes our mental, emotional, and physical resources. By going completely through the grieving process, though, our resources will eventually be restored.

None of us are immune to feeling depressed when grieving or mourning our losses. We feel helpless and think there is no hope that life will improve. As you grieve, the emotions will gradually lessen, allowing you to experience peace and joy again. If your grieving continues without subsiding or gets to the point where you cease most activities and people who care about you suggest you get help, you may be experiencing "major depression." Grieving and depression can overlap, but they aren't the same. If you feel you might be in depression, consider seeking help from your doctor, a trusted friend, or a trained counselor. Author and counselor Leslie Vernick offers these differences between grieving and depression:

> Healthy people face loss with deep sadness, even some anger, but they don't experience a reduction of self-esteem or feelings of worthlessness so characteristic of depression. It's important that we not confuse depression with the normal grieving process, although some of the symptoms (such as insomnia, sadness, and helpless feelings) may overlap…Depending on the severity of the loss, the process of mourning may last for a long

time, but eventually the grieving person begins to feel better and wants to move forward with her life.[3]

Two factors that impact our ability to heal and move forward are 1) giving ourselves plenty of time, and 2) creating the right conditions.

Giving Ourselves Plenty of Time

Making compost for my garden is never an overnight experience. It can take a few months—and even more than a year if I don't frequently turn over the organic material composting.

Like the composting process, grieving takes time, especially when the loss is significant. More than 20 years ago, after a recurrence of cancer, a divorce, and the termination of my job because I was too ill to work, I was convinced my life would never improve. It took me years to grieve and work through all the hurt and pain. The loss of my husband, my financial security, and the lifestyle I enjoyed were three of the significant losses that came with the destruction of life as I knew it.

TRASH TALK

[God] lifts the poor from the dust and the needy from the garbage dump. He sets them among princes, placing them in seats of honor.

1 SAMUEL 2:8 NLT

There were many days when I didn't want to get out of bed because of the crippling emotional pain. I wanted to pull the covers over my head and die. I had been given a two percent chance to be alive in 10 years because of the cancer. I told my concerned friends I wasn't afraid to die as much as I was afraid to live because I didn't know how I would ever move past the heartache and pain. But with God's help, time, and the support of family and friends, I slowly worked through the grieving process. I discovered some important principles on my journey that I'd like to share with you:

Grief is a time to...

• feel your sadness, disappointment, anger, frustration, shame, and everything else you're experiencing.

• say no to all but the most important activities (such as going to work and taking care of your family). Grief is not a time to achieve, produce, and perform.

• finds ways to express your thoughts and feelings through activities such as writing, journaling, painting, dancing, and talking to someone.

If you've faced a difficult loss I'm sure you've noticed that our society encourages us to ignore or hide our pain. Our lives may be falling apart, but as long as we're functioning, the people around us are fine. But if we become depressed, everyone tries to cheer us up. We're "allowed" a certain amount of time to be sad after life-changing events, but usually that time isn't adequate and we're told to "hurry up" and "get over it." I'm not opposed to helping someone feel better, but we have to remember that one of the reasons Jesus said, "Blessed are those who mourn, for they will be comforted" is because those who mourn are suffering (Matthew 5:4). They need comfort. They need to experience the sorrow and not put on a happy face. As Ecclesiastes says, there is "a time to weep and...a time to mourn" (Ecclesiastes 3:4).

Creating the Right Conditions

Creating the right environment influences our ability to make good compost and our ability to work through our grief in healthy ways. If the dead organic material in my backyard is exposed to too much air, for instance, the pile may dry out, killing some of the microorganisms that are transforming the compostable material. This drastically affects the rate of decomposition.

A good example of how the environment affects this process is to compare the length of time it takes for a banana peel to decompose in different areas. In a desert it can take up to two years.[4] Where I live in Pensylvania, it takes a few months at the most. And some websites say it only takes two to five weeks.

To create the best conditions for processing your sorrow, it's important to understand that each person approaches grief differently. The manner in which you grieve will be different from the way your best friend handles her loss. You might prefer time by yourself to sort things out, while she wants to be around a lot of people and talk through her feelings. You're both grieving, but it looks different.

What Is Your Grieving Style?

Each person has his or her own way of facing sorrow and processing pain, depending a lot on personality. Using the four personality types taught by Florence and Marita Littauer in their book *Wired That Way*, let's look at how each personality tends to approach adversity and cope with loss. The four personalities are "Popular Sanguines," "Perfect Melancholies," "Powerful Cholerics," and "Peaceful Phlegmatics."

Popular Sanguines are the outgoing, high-energy, creative people. They are imaginative, wonderful storytellers, and have the ability to make dull occasions exciting. Perfect Melancholies, on the other hand, are gifted organizers and great with details. They are wonderful listeners because they're sensitive to the needs and feelings of others. You can easily identify Powerful Cholerics because they're the natural leaders. Decisive and goal-oriented, they're not afraid to take on challenges. You'll recognize the Peaceful Phlegmatics as relaxed, easygoing people who are cooperative and supportive of others. They are consistent and work well under pressure.

Let's identify the causes of depression in each of the four personalities and follow up with a more detailed discussion on how each one prefers to handle grief.

Popular Sanguines feel depressed when life is no longer fun, and they feel isolated or disconnected from others.

Perfect Melancholies become depressed when life is far from perfect, and they see no hope of organizing or improving the situation.

Powerful Cholerics get depressed when life seems out of control. They will try to gain the upper hand in a situation until they realize there is nothing they can do, and then they may tumble into a pit of despair.

Troubling times bring too many problems for *Peaceful Phlegmatics*. Rather than getting the peace and quiet they love, they suddenly are thrown into conflict and chaos, which may trigger a depressed mood or disconnection.

As you read over the following general preferences of each personality, determine the two that most closely describe you. (Most of us are stronger in two of the personalities, with one that dominates.)

Popular Sanguines

Popular Sanguines are fun-loving, outgoing, high-energy people. Their basic desire in life is having fun. When life isn't fun, they get depressed. Of the four personalities, Popular Sanguines especially struggle with being hospitalized, going to funerals, and caring for someone over an extended period of time. Let's face it—those experiences aren't anything close to fun or exciting.

As extroverts, their emotional batteries are recharged around people. When grieving, it helps if Sanguines can talk through their losses and share their latest stories. During emotionally fragile times, Sanguines especially need attention, affection, and approval.

Nicole, a Sanguine whose son committed suicide a year ago, shared how she received a lot of calls, cards, and flowers in the weeks after her son's death. "But now I feel like everyone has forgotten about me," she said. What she found most helpful in working through her pain was to join a grief support group, regularly visit a counselor, and spend time with her family. It was important for her to be around people who would encourage her and add some lighthearted humor to counteract the seriousness of what was happening in her life.

If you are a Sanguine going through a difficult time, begin heal-ing by making a list of activities you enjoy. What brings you a sense of relief and distracts you, even briefly, from the problems you face? If you haven't had fun for a long time, this may be a tough assign-ment. Set up a time to brainstorm with a friend. If you enjoy having lunch with close friends at new restaurants in town, make a con-scious effort to carve out the space and time needed to do that. You need to do something that will put at least a hint of joy into your life. You also need some freedom in your schedule to nurture the spontaneous part of your personality. These moments of respite will enable you to better work through the painful emotions that come with unwanted change.

Perfect Melancholies

Perfect Melancholies take life seriously and desire perfection and organization. They can get depressed when life isn't perfect and there appears no way to straighten things out. The Melancholy emotion-ally needs sensitivity to his or her feelings, as well as silence and space to think. As introverts, they are emotionally recharged by solitude.

Missy's husband was killed in an automobile accident, leaving her to raise their three teenage daughters. Legal concerns and the responsibilities for the house and family overwhelmed Missy. She desperately needed time to be alone and work through her feelings. One day she confided to a friend, "I desperately want some silence. Time to think. Time to feel. But it doesn't exist at this house. The girls either have the TV on or are arguing about something."

Her friend offered to stay with the girls for a weekend to give Missy the much-needed opportunity to get away by herself and emotionally recharge.

"I spent that weekend praying, crying, journaling, and seeking God's wisdom for all the decisions I had to make," Missy shared. "It was just what I needed."

As a Melancholy, what can you do to help yourself? Because of your sensitivity, find someone who will listen to you compassionately.

When you're overwhelmed with sorrow, you need tenderness and grace. Find someone who won't always try to cheer you up or fix your problem. Find someone who will provide warmth and comfort.

Avoid getting stuck in a "poor me" mentality. Cultivate a heart of gratitude and recognize what you still have of value.

Reestablishing a routine, such as exercising every Monday, Wednesday, and Friday, may be helpful. Also schedule time to be alone. Not just a few minutes but stretches of time to read, write, journal, and go deep within. One Melancholy, who grieved the end of her engagement, said, "I must have filled at least 10 journals during that time. I poured out my disappointments, my regrets, my pain, and my anger."

While silence and space renew your mental and emotional resources, be careful not to become too disconnected from others. Total isolation is dangerous to anyone who is grieving.

Because the Perfect Melancholy loves organization and perfection, any little deed or action that will help you move in that direction will give you a sense of hope for improvement and progress. When my cancer treatments that sapped my energy lasted for more than a year, my desk and drawers became disorderly. Finding simple things like the stapler became a chore. Although I didn't have the strength to really organize things, I didn't lose my desire to have them in order. A close friend volunteered to help me get my house back together. Once a week or so she'd spend an hour or two cleaning a closet or a few drawers. It was a slow process, but I had more energy and slept better knowing my home was gradually getting organized.

Sometimes when our lives are turned upside down, we Melancholies have to lower our high standards and accept things the way they are. It's not realistic to think we can always have our drinking glasses lined up in perfect rows.

Powerful Cholerics

Powerful Cholerics are dynamic, natural-born leaders. Their basic desire is for control, which means they get depressed when life is out of control and they can't do anything about it.

Cholerics often struggle with expressing sorrow because they don't like to weep and wail at all. They like to conquer their problems and do something to regain a sense of control. They want to be powerful, not weak and helpless. This is one reason why Cholerics really struggle with the loss of health or anything else important.

I heard one Choleric who lost his business say, "I'm a stable, logical person—not crazy. Why do I feel like I'm losing it?" The problem was he realized things were out of his control and he *was* losing control. Cholerics hate that feeling.

When Jade's husband gambled away their retirement savings, she said, "I just need to get my life back to normal and be strong in the Lord." Even when Christ is the source of your strength, immediately getting your life back to normal isn't possible when it's been shattered. Rather than fight all the intense emotions you're experiencing, as a Choleric realize that after any difficult loss comes a time of mourning. While wallowing in despair isn't your style, give yourself permission to grieve.

At first Jade refused to cry or talk about her feelings, but as time went on she realized that drawing her strength from the Lord didn't mean she wouldn't suffer. She came to understand that while going through the pain is much more difficult short-term, it was the only way to growth and healing. She discovered that "when you're weak, then you're strong," which is a lesson Cholerics prefer to avoid.

As a Powerful Choleric, what can you do when you're depressed? Find areas where you can be proactive. Even deciding what you will eat for dinner or which movie to watch will empower you and help restore a sense of control. If you do have the ability to work harder, exercise longer, or start a new project, do it. A sense of accomplishment can do much to help lift your spirits.

Be careful that you don't set unrealistic expectations. Waiting is difficult because you like immediate results. Recognize the obstacles you're facing and acknowledge anything that indicates you're making progress. Because you will work to improve a situation, you may need someone to gently remind you that you're up against a problem that can't be fixed. Although you're great at tackling challenging situations, remember that sometimes you need to surrender what you're experiencing to God.

Peaceful Phlegmatics

Peaceful Phlegmatics are gentle, relaxed, easygoing people whose basic desire is for peace. Troubling times bring too many problems for this personality, who gets depressed and usually tries to ignore, escape, give up, or give in when life is difficult.

Peaceful Phlegmatics tend to share very little during tough times. They have a tendency to build walls around themselves or stuff their emotions. Savannah, who experienced several miscarriages in a row said, "I really don't like to talk about my problems. I don't want to bother anyone with my pain, so I just stuff it inside."

Unfortunately, Phlegmatics expend tremendous amounts of energy when they internalize their feelings. This adds to their already depressed level of energy. Like the Melancholy, the Phlegmatic is an introvert recharged by solitude.

If you're a Phlegmatic, find ways to get the peace and quiet you need because being around people all day can be exhausting. Amid the turmoil, it's okay to pull away for a time and do something restful you enjoy, such as reading, fishing, sitting in the park and watching the comings and goings at a birdbath, playing your guitar, or even putting on earphones and listening to quiet, soothing music. Think "temporary escape," with temporary being the key. You may need a friend to encourage you to do this as your natural tendency is to take care of everyone but yourself.

One of the biggest things you can do for yourself during difficult times is to keep things simple and give yourself plenty of time to make decisions. When you feel overwhelmed with the problems that come with unwanted change, ask, "What is one thing I need to deal with right now?" Focus on that. When it has been completed, ask, "What is the next thing I need to take care of?"

Justin used this approach when he lost his job. "I was so overwhelmed that I almost shut down emotionally. My therapist helped me gain clarity on where I needed to focus my energy. I usually try to push things under the rug, especially if it means confronting someone and dealing with conflict. My therapist helped me face my problems, as well as the pain I was experiencing."

Blair's husband had become addicted to pornography, which destroyed their marriage. As she grieved she said, "I would try to find a quiet spot where I could be alone. Sometimes I walked on the beach; at other times I rode my bike or journaled. There were many days when I was overwhelmed with grief. I just wanted to lie down and quit. But instead of giving up, I learned to rest and wait until I gathered enough strength to begin again. If I look back over this past year, I can see that I made real progress. I still have a long way to go, but at least now I'm not ignoring my problems."

When we're grieving, our emotions are raw and our differences are magnified. Give yourself permission to handle your sorrows in a way that is helpful to you. Remember that old saying that "the grass is always greener on the other side of the fence"? I've found the grass is usually greener where it is given what it needs: sunlight, water, lime, and nitrogen.

What do you or the people in your life need during times of distress? An opportunity for excitement in the midst of pain? A chance to withdraw and sort things out? Time to work or exercise harder? Moments to pull away from the reality of life to quietly rest? Providing for these needs during difficult times may be the difference between continuing to hurt and beginning to heal.

When Is Your Compost Ready?

I know my pile has transformed into black gold when it has decomposed into a crumbly, earthlike material that can easily be mixed with garden soil. You will know your losses are *starting to change* into rich nutrients for your growth when you are *no longer...*

- living with a sense of numbness or tearfulness.

- debilitated by the intensity of your pain and sadness.

- defined by the tragic experience.

- waking up in the middle of the night anxious or with a deep ache inside.

Depending on what you lost, it may take years to fully grieve and really begin anew because we can only process pain a little bit at a time. While the exact length of time varies with each person, there does come a time when the sharpness of the pain subsides. The pain may never disappear, but you will reach a point where you can accept what has happened (which doesn't mean you have to like it).

You will know your losses have composted when you're ready to integrate what was of value in your life *before* the unwanted change with what you gained by *going through* the pain of the experience. You'll find you are able to...

- resume most of your normal activities or interests. If you can't resume normal activities because you suffered a physical loss, you begin to reconstruct your life around the new parameters.

- experience moments of laughter and joy.

- let go of what is no longer part of your life.

- look to your future with hope.

- trust God with your life at a deeper level.

- identify ways you have been transformed for the better by your loss.

- experience a new sense of meaning and purpose.

Because we all experience unwanted change, we must ultimately answer this question:

"What will I do with my loss and pain?"

What will your answer be? Will you throw your losses into the trash, or will you use them to make compost? Will you allow the pain to destroy you, or will you let it transform you? The choice is yours. The only way pain and loss will produce something of value is if you persevere and work through the issues, grieve, and allow God to transform your sorrow into treasure, into "black gold."

When I'm facing one final ending after another and feel like my life is over, I remind myself that these losses will one day give me more compost. And more compost means a vibrant and beautiful garden in the future. That's when I say a prayer similar to this one:

> *Lord, show me how to make something rich and beautiful out of this destruction. Show me how to make it count for something positive. In your name I pray. Amen.*

In my book *A Gift of Mourning Glories* I wrote about the loss of my health, job, and marriage:

> Life brings losses, but the image of the compost pile keeps me from feeling totally hopeless. I have seen the rich soil that comes from dead plants, leaves, cut grass and scraps of fruit and vegetables...And I have seen how God can take our suffering and with time, patience and faith produce fertile soil for a new life.

> Although I wouldn't have said this in the midst of my troubles, I now know that I gained far more than I lost. When you allow God to guide you through life's painful processes, he gives you gifts such as peace, inner strength, wisdom, and joy—the joy of knowing him more intimately than you ever could have without the suffering. These gifts are eternal and can never be taken away.

TIME TO TAKE OUT THE TRASH

Although grieving a loss or shattered dream is painful, it's so much healthier when we acknowledge that it does hurt. Grieving is what causes the losses in our lives to slowly be transformed into rich, fertile nutrients for growth.

1. List some of the losses you've experienced. Note if you've grieved the unwanted changes. If you haven't, how will you begin?

2. Understanding that each personality copes with adversity differently can help you avoid many misunderstandings in relationships. Much tension can be alleviated when you allow everyone, including yourself, to grieve in their own ways. Identify your personality type and how you prefer to handle difficult times. Do you...

   ☐ like to be around lots of people and talk things out?

   ☐ prefer time alone to process your emotions?

   ☐ like to take on a new project or complete a current one that you have some control over?

   ☐ prefer to restrict your commitments or find a quiet place to withdraw and recharge?

3. People in our lives are going to handle their losses differently, especially if they have different personalities than we do. Write down the names of your family members and close friends, and then note what you believe their personality types are. Do they prefer to handle their grief the fun way (Popular Sanguines), the

right way (Perfect Melancholies), their way (Powerful Choler-ics), or the easy way (Peaceful Phlegmatics)?

4. Thinking back, when you experienced small and great losses in your life, what ways did you grow? Check how you grew and explain.

   ☐ courage, sensitivity, or tolerance:

   ☐ compassion for others who are going through what you've gone through before:

   ☐ faith and trust in God:

   ☐ competency in new skills you were forced to learn:

   ☐ a new career or a new ministry:

   ☐ greater love for God and other people:

   ☐ thankfulness for what you still have:

   ☐ thankfulness for God's provisions:

   ☐ your perspective of what's truly important:

☐ Other (describe):

☐ Other (describe):

9

What Emotional Clutter Is Consuming Your Life?

Have you searched a drawer so crammed with stuff that you couldn't find the one thing you wanted? I recently opened the junk drawer in my kitchen to get a clothespin to close a potato chip bag. Since I saw everything but what I wanted, I cleaned out the drawer. I found the clothespin!

To give you an idea of how jammed that junk drawer was, here's a *partial* list of what was stuffed into it: a pair of reading glasses, pens and pencils, a Sharpie marker, two pairs of scissors, a flashlight, corroded batteries, old keys, five packets of flower food, three key chains, three pairs of latex gloves, a snack bag filled with twist ties, several milk bottle lids, pot holders, rubber bands, and pictures that used to be on the refrigerator.

Thankfully, cleaning a drawer isn't too difficult and provides immediate results. But not all things that need to be cleaned are so easy. One summer I tackled my garage, and that was a totally different experience. My goal was to fit my son's car alongside mine in the two-car garage. That meant I had to empty the cluttered side. I quickly discovered that *deciding* to clean out and reorganize a large area was one thing, and *doing it* was another. As I stood looking at shelves packed with stuff and piles of flower pots, baskets, jars, cans of paint, tools, fertilizers, and sprays, I became overwhelmed.

For years, instead of discarding or giving away things, I'd chosen to store the extras and unused portions on large garage shelves. When those shelves became full, I bought larger shelves. When those got full, I started putting things on the floor in front of the shelves. We both know where this story is going, but it was such a gradual process over so many years that I didn't realize what a huge project I was creating.

I tell myself that one of the reasons I hold on to so many things is because my parents grew up during the Depression. They taught me to keep almost everything. They said, "Don't throw that out. Someday you may need it. You just never know when it might come in handy." Another reason for accumulating clutter was that I started letting things pile up after my divorce. I was trying to eliminate emotional emptiness by filling up my physical environment.

Regardless of the reasons, after several weeks of good intentions but no progress on the garage, I felt defeated. I decided the best way for me to tackle the job would be to work on it a little bit at a time. An hour here and there would give me time to think about what to throw out, what to give away, and what to keep. The added benefit of this approach was that it would help me avoid giving up and just tossing everything in the trash.

The garage project took five months. What an eye-opening experience! I realized how many things I'd held on to that I should have removed years earlier. And now not only do I have more space—enough for *two* cars in the garage—but I also have more energy, more joy, and even more money since I know what I have so I don't have to buy more.

And now I'm on a mission. As a newly self-proclaimed "Declutter Queen," my goal is to tackle every room in my home. After 35 years in one house, I'm sure I have plenty to keep me busy for quite a while.

The Costs of a Cluttered Mind and Heart

Our garages, drawers, desks, and even entire rooms aren't the only victims of disorganization. We often let emotional issues, such as worries, insecurities, secrets, shame, and guilt, gradually take over our minds and hearts, especially during times of stress and upheaval. Neglecting to clean out this kind of mess can cost us dearly. Emotional clutter paralyzes us, hinders our ability to connect with others, and may eventually crowd God out of our lives.

TRASH TALK

So throw all spoiled virtue and cancerous
evil in the garbage. In simple humility, let our
gardener, God, landscape you with the Word,
making a salvation-garden of your life.

JAMES 1:21 MSG

Emotional Clutter Paralyzes

One of the problems I had while writing this chapter was that I had too many thoughts and stories to choose from. For most of the chapters in this book I collected and filled one file folder with ideas. For this chapter, I had seven. For days I couldn't write anything because I kept rereading my notes, trying to decide which stories to keep and which to discard. One afternoon, in an effort to make some progress, I spread the file folders out on my dining room table and started to put my ideas into logical order. That's when I accidentally knocked several folders off the table. My notes scattered over the floor. I didn't know whether to laugh or cry, but one thing was certain—I was even more confused than when I started.

Apparently I'm not the only one who becomes incapacitated when presented with lots of information. Barry Schwartz, a Swarthmore College professor of social theory, studied the psychology of choice and found that too many choices can paralyze us. In one of his studies he found that the more 401(k) retirement saving plans a company offered their employees, "the more likely people were to choose no plan at all. They lost money because they were too overwhelmed by the excess of choice." Schwartz found that people spent lots of time trying to find the perfect plan, and even when they finally made a decision, they questioned their choice. His research shows "it's hard to make fear-free, guilt-free, regret-free choices when you're faced with so many."[1]

All kinds of information—whether it is in the form of worrisome thoughts, self-condemning whispers, secrets, guilt, or the millions of things we think we need to do—swirl around in our minds, drain us of valuable energy, and cause us to shut down mentally, emotionally, and physically.

Clutter Hinders Our Ability to Connect

Years ago, in the midst of a hectic week, I met a friend for breakfast. We see each other twice a year and always enjoy reconnecting. We usually start right where we left off from our last visit. This time, however, we didn't mesh. I wasn't sure what was wrong, but I knew we weren't clicking. A few times when I paraphrased back to her what I thought she was communicating, I was way off. At one point she looked down and adjusted her watchband. I thought she might be in hurry.

"Do you need to leave?" I asked.

"No," she said.

"Well, then tell me what you're going to do now that your daughter has graduated from high school."

"I need to do some purging," she said, proceeding to talk about reorganizing things in her home.

The word "purge" jumped out at me. What a descriptive word!

All week long I'd struggled to find just the right words for a writing project, and I thought "purge" communicated so much. I grabbed a note card out of my purse and wrote down the word. Then I asked her another question with my pen poised to capture her thought.

She felt offended and told me so. "Georgia, I feel like you are doing a formal interview instead of chatting with me as a friend."

Although that wasn't my intent, as I noticed my pen and note card in my hands, I understood why she felt that way. I felt guilty for appearing so impersonal. Within moments tears streamed down my cheeks as I shared the fears, worries, and concerns that were wearing me down. Once that junk was cleared out of the way, I realized I was able to listen to her intently, and we connected like old times.

This incident reminded me once again how anxieties can consume us and harm our relationships. We become so preoccupied with our concerns that we aren't able to relate in a real and intimate way. "Purge" is a descriptive word we all need to remember to prevent clutter from blocking our communication. We need to eliminate junk from our hearts and minds if we want to connect fully with others.

Clutter May Crowd Out God

Emotional clutter can harm more than our relationships with friends, family, and co-workers. Our relationship with God can suffer too. Oswald Chambers writes, "It is incredible what enormous power there is in simple things to distract our attention away from God."[2] Even simple tasks such as preparing a meal or entertaining friends can distract us if we give them too much of our emotional energy.

The biblical story of Martha and Mary is an example of how distractions can crowd out our ability to connect with Jesus. In the story Martha got so off track that she started to pick a fight with her sister:

> Martha *was distracted* by the big dinner she was preparing. She came to Jesus and said, "Lord, doesn't it seem unfair to you that my sister just sits here while I do all the work? Tell her to come and help me."
>
> But the Lord said to her, "My dear Martha, you are worried and upset over all these details! There is only one thing worth being concerned about. Mary has discovered it, and it will not be taken away from her" (Luke 10:40-42 NLT).

I heard someone speak about these verses and explain that the word "distraction" refers to a "crowd in our mind." A crowd aptly describes all the concerns that clutter our thoughts and hearts and divert our attention away from God.

Whether our emotional clutter crowds out the voice of God, hinders our ability to connect with others, or paralyzes us, we need to take it seriously and remove what isn't necessary and what doesn't belong.

Kinds of Heart and Mind Clutter

Like our jammed-full junk drawers, our hearts and minds are packed with all sorts of things, including insecurities and feelings of rejection, jealousy, and greed. How can we clear out some of this stuff? By looking at the common kinds of clutter—lies, guilt and shame, worries, and people-pleasing—and discovering how they can be purged.

Lies

We all believe some lies about ourselves. The psalmist warns, "Be careful what you think, because your thoughts run your life" (Proverbs 4:23 NCV). I recently read a story that exemplifies this truth. A young woman who grew up in an abusive home thought she was nothing but trash. She told herself, "'If you're trash, you might as well do trashy things.' So she did. Again and again. Better to believe she was garbage and act on it than risk hoping at all for something better."[3] Thankfully, she met a group of Christians who, like Jesus, accepted her just as she was and helped her see the truth.

Like each one of us, this woman *had* trash—things she needed to discard. But that in no way *made her* trash. Scripture tells us we are each a treasure to God!

Many women believe the lie that they have no voice—their opinions don't matter. Some men and women believe they'll never be good enough. Others believe they're failures (rather than having failed at something). People can also feel worthless. When one of my friends was a little girl, she overheard her grandmother say that her father wouldn't pay $30 a month for her child support. For years my friend believed the lie that she wasn't even worth a dollar a day. Some people grew up believing they were bad like I did. I was told I was bad, and so I thought that was the truth. In fact, I started to tell myself the same thing, which reinforced that wrong belief.

TRASH TALK

Every time you feel hurt, offended, or rejected, you have to dare to say to yourself: "These feelings, strong as they may be, are not telling me the truth about myself. The truth, even though I cannot feel it right now, is that I am the chosen child of God, precious in God's eyes, called the Beloved from all eternity, and held safe in an everlasting embrace."

HENRI J.M. NOUWEN

When my son was a toddler I still believed I was bad—a bad mother now. What else would a bad little girl grow up to be? Any time I didn't wisely handle Kyle or his discipline, I would obsess over my inadequacies. Being a perfectionist, I could only see two options: I was a perfect mother or I was a bad mother. As long as I continued to focus on my faults and believe those lies, I was going to live them out. Fortunately, Kyle's preschool teacher encouraged me in parenting and helped me see another option: I could be a good mother even if I could never be a perfect one.

We can acknowledge our weaknesses, mistakes, and sins without giving them our devoted attention. As bestselling author and researcher Marcus Buckingham writes,

> The more attention you pay to what's wrong with your marriage, your work, your life, yourself, the more "what's wrong" expands. Even though you are paying attention to "what's wrong" for the right reason—you want to fix

it—the more you investigate it, talk about it, relive it, explain it, the more detail the "what's wrong" acquires. And with the detail come weight and meaning and significance…Your life feels like a junkyard pile of mistakes, regrets, and fear. You find yourself being characterized by everything you're not. The weaknesses of your life *become* your life.[4]

Shame and Guilt

Shame and guilt are what we usually hide in the back corner of our closets for fear of losing the respect of others. We try to bury them underneath everything else. But no matter how many wonderful things we do, no matter how many ways we attempt to compensate for our shame or guilt, we know it exists. These two feelings are especially hazardous to our emotional and spiritual health. They can drive us crazy. Since none of us are immune to this type of painful clutter, it's important we discover how to handle them.

"By definition, shame makes you feel really bad. It's far more than embarrassment—it's a profound sense of condemnation about who you are. It's a desire to hide because there are things you don't want anyone to know."[5]

In contrast, guilt is the remorse we experience as a result of either doing something wrong or feeling as if we have done something wrong.

Shame and guilt can be authentic or false. Authentic shame and guilt are experienced when we've done something that doesn't meet God's standards or our own. Let's say you're married and have an affair. You know from Scripture that adultery isn't God's will for your life so you feel shame and guilt about your choice. The emotions are so strong that you end the affair because you no longer want to live a double life. Authentic shame can produce real remorsefulness and the desire to make amends and change.

Another example of authentic shame is related to a lapse in standards you've set. If you stopped smoking for almost a year but started again, you might feel ashamed and be motivated to correct the recent change in your behavior.

False shame and guilt, on the other hand, can be the result of *what was done to us*. Victims of abuse often feel deep shame and guilt even though they did nothing wrong. Sometimes the authentic and false versions of shame and guilt overlap. During a spiritual retreat, two of us stayed with a third friend at her lovely home in Palm Springs. One night as I was warmly snuggled in bed I decided to touch up my nail polish. While working on my nails I accidentally spilled a bit of polish on the floral bedspread. While the polish, a deep fuchsia, did match some of the colors in the floral bedspread, it was obvious that the polish was an unwanted addition.

I panicked. I quickly tried to blot the polish out, but it was still there. While I felt legitimate shame and guilt for being so careless, I also was hounded by the voices of false shame and guilt from the past: *You are bad, and this shows it. Your friend was nice enough to share her home with you, and now you've ruined her lovely bedspread. You don't deserve to have friends. You don't deserve to live.*

Since I knew I wasn't going to sleep anytime soon, I tiptoed to the room of the other guest, Linda, and quietly knocked. When she said, "Come in," I went in and shared what had happened. She got up and tried to remove the polish with a bit of remover but had no luck. She could see I was badly shaken and almost physically sick about the mishap.

"Georgia, it was an accident. Betty will understand. I can see you're really upset. Do you want to talk about this?" Linda asked.

For the next hour-and-a-half, Linda listened, talked, and prayed with me. We exposed the old "I'm a bad person" lie I'd been telling myself. We talked about what was true: I make mistakes, but God loves me unconditionally just as I am. He can and will redeem even my worst blunders. I have dear friends, such as Betty and Linda, who like me regardless of my brokenness and anxiety. That night Linda and I read several Scriptures, including 1 Peter 5:7: "Cast all your anxiety on [God] because he cares for you."

As we worked on exposing false guilt and shame, I got out my journal and recorded the lies I'd been believing: "I'm bad." "I'm a disappointment to God." "I don't deserve to be treated with respect after what I did." "I deserve to die." Then I crossed them all out with a big X and wrote over them "L-I-E." Next I wrote what was true: "I make mistakes but I take responsibility for the messes I create" and "God cares for me even when I do stupid things." As I was writing I turned the page of my journal, and there on the next page was a handwritten verse, Proverbs 14:2 MSG: "An honest life shows respect for GOD."

Linda had given me the journal a year earlier. As she often does, she'd written different verses God had given her on random pages throughout the blank book. When I pointed out the verse, we both smiled and laughed because we were experiencing God in a real way, and I'd also just admitted that I'd been tempted to turn the bedspread over to cover up the accident.

<hr>

TRASH TALK

A clean conscience is a soft pillow.

GERMAN PROVERB

<hr>

Uncovering my false shame made all the difference in giving me peace of mind and the ability to sleep that night. The next morning Linda and I prayed again as I mustered up the courage to tell Betty what I'd done. She wasn't upset at all, which underscored even more the healing power of confessing our junk. At that moment I was truly free of any emotional pain from that incident and what it brought up from the past.

That story is a good example of how shame works. If it had been my own bedspread, I might have become angry at myself for being careless, but I wouldn't have felt shame. Shame often arises when we fear someone is disapproving or judging us as stupid, foolish, unworthy, unlovable, or bad. I feared Betty's judgment. Once I shared with Linda and felt her grace (not judgment!), I had the courage to confess to Betty.

Recently while I was waiting for a flight home at the airport, I spilled some hot tea on the floor in a bookstore. I didn't have any tissues or napkins to wipe it up, so I went over and told the two clerks at the counter what I'd done. Immediately they called someone to clean it up. "Thank you for telling us," one clerk said. The other nodded her head and smiled. "You don't know how many people do that and don't say anything to us. Then someone slips on it and maybe gets hurt. We really appreciate you saying something."

I understand why people walk away. When I first realized I couldn't clean the tea up on my own, I wanted to pretend it didn't happen. No one else was standing there to see it happen, so I could "get away with it." But concealing it would have created guilt for not doing what I knew I should (authentic guilt) and I'd have to deal with that eventually. Since "our lives are always colored by guilt—guilt about things we have done wrong, guilt about things we have not done at all, and guilt, at times, simply about being alive, healthy and experiencing life's pleasures,"[6] we need to remove it so its clutter won't "rob us of the spirit of our own lives…and of the consolation of God."[7]

I encourage you to "own your guilt and shame" so you can disown it. Refuse to be a victim by allowing those emotions to control you. And if you feel you have hidden shame and guilt, find someone safe, accepting, and trustworthy to help you uncover the hidden junk in all its ugliness then steer you to the truth of God's love. I have a few precious friends who will do that for me. They know my garbage, and still they love me. They also know that allowing shame and guilt to clutter my heart and mind can crowd out God's love and peace and pull me away from my relationship with Christ. My friends are quick to remind me that I can come boldly to the throne of God's grace and receive his mercy and help when I need it. Hebrews 4:16 says, "So let's walk right up to him and get what he is so ready to give. Take the mercy, accept the help."

Does the brokenness and pain that comes from your shame and guilt remain and bring even more pain? Why not let your brokenness and shame lead to change? Clean out that closet clutter, whether it is something you did, you didn't do, or was done to you and give it to the God who loves you and offers healing and freedom.

Worry

Worry is another clutter-maker that has no business in our hearts and minds. We worry about losing our jobs, our retirement savings, our health, our marriages, our homes, and even our youthfulness. Worry leaves us weary and exhausted. As Corrie ten Boom said, "Worry does not empty tomorrow of its sorrow; it empties today of its strength."

When we worry we put fear in the place of God. We are essentially doubting that God is in control of our lives, and we're questioning whether he can and will take care of us.

When you feel worry or fear, ask, "What's the worst thing that could happen?" Also ask, "What are my options?" Explore your choices—what actual influence you have over the situation and what is out of your control. Do what you can (even if you are terrified of doing it), detach emotionally if possible, and release it to God, remembering all the good things he has done for you in the past. God will keep you in perfect peace when your thoughts are fixed on him and you trust in him (Isaiah 26:3).

My favorite verse on how to handle worry is Philippians 4:6-7 NLT:

> Don't worry about anything; instead, pray about everything. Tell God what you need, and thank him for all he has done. Then you will experience God's peace, which exceeds anything we can understand. His peace will guard your hearts and minds as you live in Christ Jesus.

People Pleasing

If we're honest, most of us will admit to caring more about pleasing our spouses, children, and bosses than we do about pleasing

God. We yearn for their approval and respect. But in John 12:43 we are warned not to care so much for the approval, compliments, or praise of people: "When push came to shove they cared more for human approval than for God's glory" (John 12:43 MSG).

Needing to keep or gain the approval of the people in our lives assaults us and wears us down. We have little time and energy left to do the things God calls us to do. Setting boundaries with others can help us keep the sometimes-demanding expectations of others within limits so we have the time and space we need to be successful and happy.

It's difficult sometimes to separate your emotions about a person from the requests or demands he or she might make. If you're feeling under the gun, I encourage you to take action by setting healthy boundaries. You can even do this a little bit at a time because "action is the antidote to feeling overwhelmed."[8] The clutter of people pleasing can quickly strip you and your home of peace and joy.

Nancy Sebastian Meyer conveyed an important lesson she learned about people pleasing:

> I'm hard-wired to be a high-energy people pleaser. This means I get many calls from people who know I'm capable and willing to help. I hate to say no and disappoint people, yet saying yes is not always possible, nor is it God's will. So for many years I lived in a constant state of frustration and exhaustion—not able but trying to please everyone at all times.
>
> Then God graciously gave me a perspective shift. Several years ago someone called to ask me to help, and I knew I couldn't say yes. When I told her how sorry I was, she said, "That's totally okay. Maybe you are my *connector*. Do you know anyone else who might be able to meet this need?" A connector! Wow! I'd never thought of me in that light before.
>
> Now when someone asks me to do something, I inquire of God if I am to meet this need or how to direct this

person to the help needed instead of feeling responsible or guilty or exhausted over the situation.

Decluttering Step-by-step

The cost of neglecting emotional clutter is high, but the rewards of clearing it out are many. For starters, we have more *time* to spend with God and the people who are important for us. We have more *space* in our hearts and minds for positive emotions, such as peace, joy, and love. We have more *energy* for doing what brings us pleasure.

As I mentioned earlier, wanting to clean out my garage and doing it were two different things. Without a plan of action and the discipline to implement it, I'd still be looking at my garage clutter. I was able to make progress when I divided the big task into smaller sections. Then I focused on one item at a time, deciding whether I wanted to keep it (and where I would store it), give it away, or throw it away. Once that single item was taken care of, I focused on the next item and so on. By concentrating on one item at a time, one shelf at a time, one hour at a time, I eventually finished the job.

Similarly, our hearts and minds are jammed full of different thoughts, feelings, and attitudes, some of which are valuable and some that need to be recycled or tossed. The latter items we want to ruthlessly eliminate. Author Nancy Sebastian Meyer shared a process she discovered for dealing with the things cluttering her heart and mind:

> I recognized a huge energy drainer in my life almost by accident. Feeling discouraged and behind on several large projects, I began meeting weekly for prayer and accountability with a friend. In trying to come up with a practical way to show her what I was doing from week to week, I created a simple one-page form. I filled in my goals for the next week and gave a copy to her so she could pray very specifically for me. Then the next week, I filled in on the original sheet what I had accomplished.

I copied that sheet and also gave her a new sheet for the upcoming week.

As the weeks went by, I did much more than accomplish projects. I gained an unbelievable peace.

I have been inconsistent with this method of scheduling my life even though I know it to be essential. However, every time I go back to this goal-writing system the result is the same: less shame, less fear, less worry, more peace, and much more accomplishment.

There is more than one way to declutter. Nancy used a weekly list. Here's another idea for proactively discarding what doesn't belong:

- List your energy drainers.

- Choose one item to resolve or eliminate.

- Tell yourself the truth about that item—that it's clutter and not necessary. (Always purge emotional clutter with the truth.)

- Get help if you need or want someone to talk to and encourage you through this process.

- Enjoy the accomplishment and benefits of removing the item.

- Select the next item to tackle.

List Your Energy Drainers

What is stealing your valuable resources? What is sucking the life out of you? What's bugging you? Begin to make a list of all the things that are draining your time, energy, and ability to focus. I use the word "begin" because many times we don't recognize right away all that is cluttering our hearts and minds. We've grown accustomed to some things even though they may be costing us dearly.

Choose One Item to Resolve or Eliminate

Dealing with everything that is dragging you down at once can be overwhelming and unproductive. Look over your list and pick one issue to tackle today. One of my friends set out to clean her kitchen and realized that one drawer, which was in a very handy location—what she calls prime real estate—was filled with things she rarely used. She decided to clean out that drawer first so she could free up the valuable space that had been filled with insignificant items.

═══ TRASH TALK ═══

Identifying destructive thought patterns is a process
that usually requires the help of others. Don't be
threatened by learning painful truths about yourself.
Repentance is a change of mind or outlook. It
requires a new way of seeing things—God's way. It
begins the path to healthy and joyful living.

STEVE CORNELL

What is taking up prime real estate in your heart and mind? What will yield high dividends if removed? Why not start with that issue? If that issue is big and scary, break it down into smaller, more doable pieces. Or start with something else small to give you practice and confidence in cleaning out emotional junk.

Tell Yourself the Truth About That Item

Dejunking our hearts and minds means discarding trash thoughts and replacing them with God's truth. Sometimes we don't even recognize the lies or false shame for what they are—untruths. Don't hesitate to ask for help if you need someone to work with you to identify the emotional clutter interfering with your life.

While speaking at a retreat I was given a bookmark with this helpful comparison list adapted from Timothy Warner's book *Resolving Spiritual Conflicts & Cross-Cultural Ministry*:

Satan's Lies	God's Truth
You get your identity from what you have done.	You get your identity from what God has done for you.
You get your identity from what people say about you.	You get your identity from what God says about you.
Your behavior tells you what to believe about yourself.	Your belief about yourself determines your behavior.

I encourage you to read and memorize Scripture so you'll know God's truths. Find a verse that speaks to you and remind yourself of it frequently. For one year I meditated on Zephaniah 3:17: "The Lord your God is with you, he is mighty to save. He will take great delight in you, he will quiet you with his love, he will rejoice over you with singing." I asked friends to pray that the truth of this verse would sink deeply into my mind and heart. I also asked God to show me how he delighted in me, and I noted what he revealed in my journal.

At the end of the year I was flying across the country to meet two dear friends for a spiritual retreat. As I was deplaning, I was drawn to a beautiful little girl two rows in front of me. She was around four years old, and as her father picked her up he kissed her on the cheek and then held her tightly. I could tell the father adored his daughter. I was so mesmerized by his affection for her that I watched them walk toward their next gate until they were out of sight.

The next day my friends and I were working through Richard Foster's spiritual disciplines. One of the exercises was to pray and picture ourselves with Jesus. As I closed my eyes, I saw Jesus standing while I was prostrate at his feet like a beggar, my outstretched arms holding on to his ankles. In this image I pleaded with Jesus not to let me go. Gently Jesus bent down, picked me up, and lovingly held me up to his shoulder.

That image of Jesus—like the doting father lifting up his little girl—is what I consciously retrieve when the lies about my identity and the clutter build up and try to take over. Over the years of sharing that image, other women have shared how they picture themselves with Jesus. One young mother said she sees herself curled up like a little kitten in the palm of God's hand. Another woman visualizes herself snuggled up on Jesus' lap with her head against his chest listening to his heartbeat.

If you aren't the type of person who sees or visualizes in pictures, pray about it. Ask God to give you a lasting vision of your relationship with him. Here's a note I received after a conference where I asked people to do that:

> You said to ask Jesus for a vision of His love for me. I don't usually see "pictures" in my mind, but God gave me the image of Jesus standing with His arms outstretched to me. I ran to Him. He lifted me up and spun me around in His arms with joy and laughter. I felt He was delighting over me! This has ministered to me many times.

Images are powerful. One reason they can be so helpful is because images use the right side of our brains and words are processed on the left side. Between Scripture and the mental images, both sides of our brains are saturated with the truth. How do you see yourself? What image do you have? Ask the Lord to give you a mental picture that will drive the truth of his love home to you. Isaiah 40:11 reads, "He gathers the lambs in his arms and carries them close to his heart." Can you see Jesus holding you close to his heart and protecting you? Can you picture yourself walking beside Jesus with His arm across your shoulders?

Get Help If You Need or Want Someone to Talk To

When recycling, some items are considered hazardous and require special handling. Many old batteries were made with mercury and lead so they're considered "hazardous waste" and shouldn't be thrown out with ordinary garbage. Just as I had to take special action when getting rid of the corroded ones I found in my kitchen junk drawer, some of our emotional clutter may need special handling.

When we're trying to deal with the clutter in our hearts and minds, it's not unusual to shut down emotionally because we're overwhelmed, especially if we've allowed junk to accumulate for years. That consuming clutter didn't build up overnight, so we shouldn't expect it to be removed overnight.

If you'd like or need encouragement in handling this type of clutter, you might benefit from the services of a life coach. He or she can help you stay focused. If you find you are completely unable to move forward, you may need the support and guidance of a licensed therapist or counselor, particularly if you are experiencing a lot of emotional pain. Your church or a local Christian organization may have trained counselors or can recommend some. I do suggest you seek professional *Christian* help because you need biblical truth to successfully eliminate clutter and grow. Even one visit can do wonders to get you on the right path!

If a counselor seems too formal, a safe and trustworthy friend might be able to help you, but only if he or she is willing to ask tough questions, hold you accountable, and encourage you to continue until you succeed.

Enjoy the Accomplishment and Benefits of Removing the Item

When I clean out a closet or room, I get a sense of satisfaction and delight. I'm always amazed at how much pleasure I experience looking at completed projects, especially in contrast to the burden and weariness I feel just glancing at a messy closet. I feel lighter and freer seeing the results of my hard work.

Along that same line, getting rid of a self-condemning lie that has been dragging you down for years will bring you great joy and a true sense of peace. Enjoy that experience! Celebrate your victory by thanking God for enabling you to toss out the old thought pattern.

Select the Next Item to Tackle

After you've thoroughly enjoyed the accomplishment and benefits of removing your first emotional clutter item, decide on the next one to take on. What is crowding out God's best for your life? Why not ask God for help? "Lord, show me what is distracting me and keeping me from focusing on you, and then help me clear it out of my life." Then, in the days ahead, be aware of God's leading. When he brings to light that next piece of garbage, get the purging process started again.

Although it took me five months to clean my garage, it was definitely worth it. I feel a lightness when I'm in there now. I sleep better at night. I'm more creative and not irritated so easily. Instead of wearily looking at the mess every time I pull into the garage, I notice how nice it looks. I smile when I remember how much time and energy I used to waste trying to find a garden trowel or another tool among the mess. Life is so much easier without clutter!

Recently I asked a good friend to pray with me about an important matter. "I will," she said smiling. Then she reminded me, "Just make sure none of *your* stuff is getting in the way of hearing from God." My friend knows me well, and I knew what she meant. After all, as a new Declutter Queen, my goal is to tackle every room in my house and be intentional about clearing out the emotional clutter that weighs me down. And yes, I have plenty to keep me busy.

TIME TO TAKE OUT THE TRASH

1. We've talked about some of the things that can clutter our hearts and minds. Besides being consumed with lies, shame, guilt, insecurities, and worries, what issues paralyze you and create disconnects in your relationships (for instance, envy, perfectionism, comparing yourself to others)?

2. Are there any thoughts and feelings that consume you and control your life? Make a list, and note how the clutter depletes your energy.

3. Remember my junk drawer full of items such as rubber bands, scissors, pens, markers, and other old stuff I'd hung on to for years? It was time for me to do some real cleaning. Look at your list of emotional clutter you wrote for question 2. What one thing are you ready to eliminate from your heart and mind, beginning today?

4. Is there anything in your emotional junk drawer that is so toxic or damaging that you should ask a trusted friend or professional for help? If yes, who will you ask? When will you contact this source of help?

5. Make a list of all the benefits you can think of for cleaning out the negative thoughts, feelings, and attitudes that clutter your mind.

10

Are You Taking Out Your Trash?

Have you ever been mesmerized by the beauty of a garden, home, or scenic view? If so, think about that breathtaking image for a moment. When visualizing that picture you probably didn't think, "This is amazing, and there's no garbage strewn around." What most likely caught your eye was the beauty, not the absence of trash.

In the same way, when you're attracted to someone who loves God first and foremost and strives to keep a pure heart, you probably don't immediately think, "That person must be routinely dealing with hurts, grudges, anger, and resentment." Instead you usually delight in who the person is. You enjoy being with him or her.

It doesn't matter if we are talking about a home, a garden, or a person. All of them require routine maintenance to stay lovely. An established garden needs regular weeding, pruning, cultivating, and fertilizing. A lived-in home needs dusting, vacuuming, and having the bathrooms and kitchen cleaned. Every person needs to maintain certain practices to keep negative emotions to a minimum and grow strong emotionally and spiritually.

Studies have shown that negative emotions are harmful to our health—even shortening our lives. As we've seen, they are also destructive to our families, our relationships, and our careers. Once the negative emotions are removed, positive ones can grow and flourish, improving our overall health and even inoculating us against illness and depression.[1]

In the first chapter of this book we talked about cultivating self-awareness and expressing our emotions in healthy ways so we will stay out of the emotional danger zone. Once this habit becomes ingrained, we need to continue with the changes we've made so we don't slip back into old patterns. Yes, it's natural to experience setbacks, to find ourselves acting out our emotions in hurtful ways occasionally. But by continuing to monitor our lives and dealing with any trash that comes our way, we can keep clutter to a minimum and any relapses will be temporary.

Let's stay focused on routinely reducing, reusing, and recycling our trash.

Seeing Our Trash

During a free afternoon at a retreat, my friend and I went for a long walk on a path by a lovely lake that led into the woods. We were totally immersed in the wonders of God's creation until suddenly we came upon a huge pile of trash in the middle of this remote, beautiful area. There was a heap of car and tractor tires, rusty wire fencing, a stuffed living room chair torn up, a ripped leather computer chair, rusty paint cans, 55-gallon plastic containers, a window-unit air conditioner, a broken doghouse, pieces of aluminum siding, and even an old toilet. Needless to say, our serene walk came to an abrupt halt. We wondered why this retreat center, which emphasized experiencing nature and God's delightful creation, would keep this trash pile alongside the woodland trail. Surely other guests and people had complained about this eyesore.

The next day I again walked the path past that pile of junk and realized it probably wasn't affiliated with the retreat center. The trash seemed to be on the property of a neighboring farm, sitting on the edge of a cultivated field. The farmhouse and barns were about a half mile away so the farmer most likely dumped the junk there to hide it from his family's view. Although it might have been out of his sight and mind, it clearly was polluting the beauty of the woodlands and impacting everyone who walked along the path.

Our emotional trash can resemble that desecration of pristine countryside. Once we begin to see our emotional trash for what it is—garbage—we are less likely to allow it to accumulate and pollute our lives and the lives of others. We'll be more sensitive to what it costs us to ignore it and more attuned to the fact that if we don't deal with our junk, other people will see it and possibly be negatively affected.

A key part of identifying our junk as it occurs, so we can deal with it as soon as possible, is to recognize the various reasons or excuses we tell ourselves for not seeing things as they are. We often justify our behaviors and attitudes, using our rationalizations to skate by the issues. And we do this even when it's obvious we're becoming walking time bombs. What are some of the ways we resist seeing our rubbish? What are some common excuses people use?

I'm entitled to feel this way. We often struggle with letting go of frustrations and resentments because we're convinced we have a right to hold on to these feelings. One friend I know did countless favors for a co-worker, but when she needed a ride home she was left hanging because the co-worker refused to help. My friend felt justified for reacting negatively about the way she was treated. After all, who wouldn't be upset when they extend compassion and concern and receive apathy and even antagonism in return?

Justified or not, normal or not, we are the ones carrying the harmful anger, resentment, and bitterness in our hearts. And just because our emotional reactions are "normal and usual" doesn't mean we're responding in a godly way. Our goal isn't to be normal; *our goal is to be godly* and free of emotional trash.

"They" deserved it. Sometimes when we're furious we take our anger out on others. We rationalize they got what they deserved.

Nina had just completed six pressure-filled weeks at work when Thanksgiving arrived. Even though she was exhausted, she and her husband decided to go ahead with the lovely holiday dinner they'd been planning for their elderly parents. Her assumption was that her husband, normally a helpful person, would share in the meal preparation and cleanup.

When the day came, however, he was consumed with eliminating a virus on his computer. When she broached the subject of preparing for the meal, he let her know how much he resented "always having to help." Within seconds, Nina verbally reacted and unloaded all the resentments she'd held on to for the last few months. She lashed out in anger about how she had to carry the brunt of the work at home *and* at the office, and that no one seemed to care enough to help her out.

Needless to say, the result was an emotionally chilly holiday weekend for Nina and her husband and an uncomfortable evening for their parents.

We usually end up paying a heavy price for indulging in reactions. We may feel guilty and ashamed of our behavior. We may say things we will later wish we could take back. And we wound others and God's heart because we've refused to acknowledge and failed to deal with our trash.

I don't have time. A friend who was repeatedly upset about the poor choices of a co-worker, said, "Because of her decisions, I end up with more work and more stress, but I don't have time to deal with her feelings or mine. I need to keep working or I'll never meet all the deadlines I have coming up over the next few months." As she talked, she kept rubbing her forehead like she had a headache.

"Oh, but you will deal with it," I told her. "The only question is where and when." I pointed to her head. "Maybe you already are."

Like this friend, sometimes we don't want to be bothered with handling the trash. It does take time to cultivate good emotional health. But failing to deal with negative feelings in the short-term makes them much worse in the long run. They eventually become the elephant in the room that everyone sees but no one talks about.

Yes, we are busy, busy people, slammed with one responsibility after another. Thinking we're too busy to deal with issues discounts the costs that will come from ignoring our upset feelings. Eventually they will demand attention and wreak havoc in our lives. The longer we put off dealing with issues, the bigger, older, and more difficult they will be to handle and the stronger the consequences may be. If we take the time now while the problems are still relatively small, we can take care of them quickly and with minimal damage.

Please note there is an important difference between "not having time" and acknowledging that "the time is not right now." Timing can be critical. Sometimes we need to put some distance between us and an issue so we can pray for and gain a godly perspective. Recently someone promised to do something for me. At the last minute she backed out. Her decision not only negatively impacted me but also affected another person. The incident was so emotionally charged that my friend and I couldn't discuss it that day without getting upset. We remained polite, but we avoided that topic knowing we might say something we'd later regret. I asked God to show me what I needed to see. The next morning my friend called and apologized. After a good night's sleep, both of us could openly talk about the issue in an unemotional way not available to us previously.

While there are times when it can be destructive to deal with a conflict immediately, the idea of not addressing our feelings at all because of lack of time is short-sighted. Laura learned this truth the hard way. "There are days when all I can do is sit on the couch, cry, and pour out my sob story to a friend because I've let everything pile up too long," she shared. "I'd be much better off if I'd dealt with all the little stuff one small chunk at a time and only lose an hour or even a few minutes instead of wasting a whole day because I'm unable to do anything *but* deal with it now."

I don't want to focus on the negative. See if you can relate to this woman's attitude: "At my house we don't talk about anything unless it's positive. It's not good to dwell on the negative, so feelings like resentment and rage aren't an issue." Just because we don't acknowledge or talk about a negative emotion or behavior doesn't mean we don't have one. While I agree that dwelling on the positive in others is important, obeying God means being open to seeing our negative emotions and unattractive behaviors.

Tony, who attends my church, grew up with a military father who ran his home like an army barracks. He didn't permit any of his eight children to express their feelings unless they were happy ones. "I kept anger, jealousy, fear, and sadness inside," Tony said. "I tried to avoid my feelings by excessive work, but they piled up anyway. And every once in a while they came out sideways through physical fights."

As an adult, Tony has learned the value of addressing his feelings—the happy ones *and* the sad ones. Doing this enables him to more easily keep his anger in check and be more authentic in his closest relationships as he lives to honor God.

I can't handle any more pain. We might resist dealing with our negative thoughts and feelings because we're already overwhelmed. We don't think we have the ability to handle any more misery. We're afraid we'll lose control or even go crazy. At those times, we may need to seek the assistance of a friend, a counselor, a pastor, or a support group. We need to allow people to help us confront the crippling heartache a little bit at a time. Talking things over with a neutral person often helps us see just how normal our emotions and reactions are.

On other occasions we might avoid distressful situations because we don't want to acknowledge our poor choices. Because of several unforeseen problems, the outstanding balance on Gail's credit card built up to the point where she was unable to handle it on her own. Gail spent months fretting about it. Although she dreaded telling her husband because she knew he would be disappointed, she finally had no choice. "I cried—and I don't cry easily. It hurt so much to admit how stupid I'd been. I knew my husband would be extremely upset—and he was. But he also helped me find a solution to the problem. I should have told him long ago and saved a lot of worry and a lot of money spent on Tums." (Because Gail's husband has never been volatile or abusive, it was the pain of exposing her mistake that she was trying to avoid. If you live with an abusive person, one of your primary goals is to stay safe.)

I don't want to navel gaze and think only about me. Self-awareness isn't the same as self-absorption. When we become self-focused, we are consumed with ourselves and obsessed with striving for perfection. Self-awareness leads us to acknowledge that we are broken people who make mistakes and mess up. Having self-awareness enables us to see we are flawed and have emotional trash. When we acknowledge that we harbor all kinds of emotions, we can surrender the junky ones to Christ, who loves us unconditionally and gives us his grace and mercy. He will show us how to manage our garbage in a way that leads to health, growth, and maturity.

TRASH TALK

Your Trash Wanted!

God is offering top blessings in exchange for
depression, anxiety, rejection, stress, resentment,
fear, anger, losses, and insecurities!
Learn how to recycle your junk and turn
that emotional trash into *treasure!*

GEORGIA SHAFFER, *TRASH TO TREASURE* SEMINAR

Recognizing our trash means taking the time to cultivate self-awareness and remove any resistances we might have to addressing our emotional issues. We want to be healthier and live more fulfilled lives. And remember, even when we try to push our junk out of sight and out of mind, it can still often be seen and felt by the people around us.

Keeping Trash to a Minimum

If we want to keep our emotional disasters to a minimum, we need to be *intentional* about removing the trash regularly. Songwriter Heather Harlan shares how she has been working to routinely reduce the amount of physical and emotional trash she accumulates:

> My family and I are now living in an environmentally conscious community, and we are working more to recycle. When we put a small waste can in each room with a recycling symbol for paper, we doubled the amount of paper we recycled. We found a box just the right size to place by the kitchen door for newspapers, disposable mail, and paper egg cartons. I hung a blue trash bag by a cabinet, out of sight, for glass and plastic recyclables.
>
> We don't have a garden, but my brother and his wife do, and they love to compost. We started saving fruit and vegetable peelings, egg shells, toilet paper tubes, and coffee grounds in a tightly covered bucket for their compost pile. It's fun to see their faces light up when I'm on an errand and drop by with a hot, steamy bucket of decaying matter. My brother happily quipped last week, "Not everyone would drive across town with a bucket of garbage for us."
>
> My family and I are delighted that we now set on the curb only one trash bag half-filled every week for pickup. Everything else is recycled. What made the difference? Intentionality. We started making decisions instead of mindlessly pitching everything...even the smelly garbage.
>
> We are looking forward to some warm, juicy tomatoes from my brother and his wife's garden later this summer, and our compost will have helped to grow them.

The word "intentionality" applies to our emotional garbage as well as our physical trash. Heather understands that connection. She goes on to say:

> Nearly every circumstance that produces negative emotions can ultimately be used if I process it with prayer and intentionality. Anger? Resentment? Shame? Guilt? I learn from feelings and events that may initially seem pretty useless in my life. As I deal with them intentionally, I find these sorting-out experiences seem to be the most consistent way the Lord produces fruit in my life. And to think, some people just throw it all out!

Being intentional to maintain routines and practices, such as prayer and reading Scripture, are important for helping us reduce the amount of junk in our lives and become more fruitful. We daily throw our physical trash away, weekly take it out to the curb, and yearly do our spring cleaning. Likewise, some of our ongoing activities, such as praying, are best done daily; attending church or meeting with our spiritual friends is weekly; and a few, such as spiritual retreats, we do on a yearly basis. The following suggestions offer practices you can put in place to recognize, remove, and recycle your trash.

Physical Practices

Our physical health impacts our emotional health, and our emotions impact our bodies. One of the best things we can do to reduce the amount of emotional trash we accumulate is to protect ourselves from total depletion. Lack of sleep and an unhealthy diet are two things that often put us in the danger zone. Are you carving out time to sleep, eat well, rest, and exercise? Burning the candle at both ends means we have fewer resources available to handle our emotions in positive ways.

One single mother told me she didn't deal with her emotions from a miscarriage for 20 years. She said,

My life was on overload. I was always running on empty and never had the ability to deal with my feelings. I never took time just to rest and renew. The price I paid was that part of me remained dead, and I didn't cope well with the ongoing hassles in my life—especially in front of my children. Now that I have been able to cry and be angry about losing that baby, I not only have a sense of closure but I'm more real in my relationships. I'm more alive.

Charles Stanley has an acronym for protecting ourselves from Satan's clutches. He uses H-A-L-T and says, "Don't allow yourself to get too **Hungry, Angry, Lonely,** or **Tired.**" When we are physically hungry or tired, we are more apt to say and do things we later regret.

Social Practices

There are times when we need to be quiet and away from the crowd or our families to sort things out. But total isolation is not healthy. Author Gary Thomas warns,

> If, as an individual or as a couple, you live a lonely life, you walk near the spiritual edge. If you walk near the edge for a long time, eventually you'll fall off. God didn't design you as a hermit, either emotionally or socially. We have to take the time, push past the hurt, make the effort, and endure the occasional pain and disappointment to engage in the holy pleasure of social interaction. Relating to others is like exercise; we may not always feel like doing it, but if we allow our reluctance to rule our response every time, we'll become very unfit—and personally, very unhappy.[2]

Building close, intimate relationships is crucial to our emotional health and growth. We need people who will encourage us when we are down, who will help us carry our burdens when we are overwhelmed with a crisis, and who will speak the truth to us in love.

We need people who will accept us just as we are but care enough to point out when we are being blind to our junk or when it is negatively impacting someone. One of the best ways to have those people in our lives is to care enough to be that kind of person for them.

Emotional Practices

God didn't create you as an emotional trash compactor. Feelings are not meant to be stuffed, crammed, or packed tightly. You need down times when you can express your deepest thoughts and feelings by talking, writing, or drawing. You need time to clean things out—no matter how many years or minutes you've held on to stuff—so your positive emotions won't be contaminated by the negative ones.

Imagine an unwashed bowl that has dried, caked-on remains of chili inside. What would happen if I use that bowl for wonderful vanilla ice cream? The flavor of the ice cream will be tainted by the old, dried-up chili. Similarly, what we place in our hearts, no matter how pure, will be contaminated by any anger, bitterness, or deep hurts lodged there. So let's make sure we routinely remove those negatives!

Libby, a woman I met at a weekend conference, told me her parents divorced when she was young. Over the years each parent remarried and divorced several times. Her home life was like a revolving door because with each new marriage came more stepbrothers and stepsisters whom Libby grew to love. And with each divorce, these brothers and sisters disappeared. Libby grew up, got married, and had two children. After eight years, she and her husband divorced. Now she is remarried and shared with me:

> I realize that what I experienced growing up is now contaminating a very beautiful relationship with my husband. I never grieved over the loss of my step-siblings. If I don't work through those feelings I will lose my husband. I've come to realize I expect to lose any close relationship, and so I unwittingly pull back. I know it isn't

going to be easy to let go of the protective mechanisms I've put in place, but at least now I'm aware of what I didn't deal with years ago.

Like Libby, we must come to realize how much our current relationships are tainted by the losses, resentments, disappointments, and insecurities we haven't dealt with from the past. We don't want those emotions to taint or destroy the good things we now have.

Pastor and author Andy Stanley suggests that we monitor our emotions daily by asking ourselves certain questions to strengthen and purify our hearts. He calls this practice "habits of the heart." In a message he gave at the International Christian Retailer's Show many years ago, he talked about routinely asking his children at prayer time: "Is everything okay in your heart? Are you mad at anyone? Did anyone say anything to hurt you? Is there someone you are jealous of?"

Andy recommends that when we are angry, we forgive. When we are greedy, it's important to give. When guilty, confess, and when jealous, celebrate with the one who is rejoicing.

TRASH TALK

It's the constant and determined effort that breaks
down resistance, sweeps away all obstacles.

CLAUDE M. BRISTOL

Spiritual Practices

Some disciplines, such as talking to God and reading his Word, are essential to our emotional health. Others, such as journaling and spiritual friendships, are activities we may find helpful.

Praying

Praying is a basic activity that is best done daily to maintain a trash-conscious lifestyle. I like how Wanda, who attended one of my conferences, put it: "My time of prayer is like Drano. It really helps to clean things out."

Jesus is the Master of Waste Management. Through the guidance of the Holy Spirit, he will show us what he will help us recycle or compost and what needs to go. Since he already knows exactly what junk we're harboring in our hearts, we can be totally honest and tell him how we feel. One person I know often begins her "trash dumping" by telling God, "I'm angry at 'X,' and I don't want to forgive. I want 'X' to suffer. Take away those feelings, Lord. And give me the desire to forgive."

Reading Scripture

When we read Scripture it's important to ask how the passage applies to us. The Bible is filled with stories that remind us of the consequences of ignoring trash. The Old Testament story of Joseph and his older brothers, which begins in Genesis 37, is a perfect example.

Israeli patriarch Jacob loved his young son, Joseph, more than his other children. Joseph's older brothers were deeply hurt, angry, and jealous that they weren't as valued. (That seems like a reasonable human response.) Perhaps at first their father's favoritism led the older brothers to overachieve. Perhaps his continued bias caused the brothers to feel hopeless and frustrated. What did it matter what they achieved or accomplished? They *never* could win their father's favor like Joseph had. Slowly jealousy toward Joseph grew and grew, eventually far beyond "ordinary" sibling rivalry. Eventually their hearts were filled with hatred. One day when the brothers were shepherding far from home, Jacob sent Joseph to make sure they were well. As they saw him approaching, they decided to seize the opportunity to kill him. (These older brothers were "living in the danger zone" and ready to act out their feelings instead of expressing them. They had accumulated a lot of trash!)

Before they carried out the plot, Reuben, the eldest brother, intervened and convinced the others to toss Joseph in a deep cistern (well) that was dried up. When Joseph arrived, the brothers carried out their plan. Before Reuben could rescue Joseph and send him home, the other brothers noticed a caravan of traders on their way to Egypt. They sold Joseph to them as a slave.

But getting rid of Joseph didn't make the brothers' lives better. Instead, their choices and actions created more stress. They had to lie to their father about Joseph's whereabouts, convincing Jacob that a wild animal had killed him. They had to watch as their father grieved his loss. They had to live with their lies and carry the heavy burden of guilt because they knew their decisions had caused their father to experience deep depression.

And, of course, their actions created many hardships for Joseph.

To get the most out of stories like this in relation to our trash, we can ask and answer questions like these:

- Is there any part of me that can relate to the feelings of the older brothers?

- Have I been deeply hurt by a parent, a boss, a co-worker, a friend who favored someone else?

- If so, how did I deal with it? And am I still dealing with it?

- If I'm angry, do I feel justified? Am I entitled to feeling this way?

- Am I allowing envy and bitterness to grow in my heart and become hatred?

Journaling

In my journal I record my written prayers and the answers I receive. It also serves as a trash heap where I dump my frustrations, irritations, worries, and anger without restriction. This helps me evaluate what's happening in a gut-honest way so I can take the steps I need to remain healthy.

A great thing about journaling is that you can write whatever comes to your mind *and* how you feel about it. If you're feeling hurt about a comment your sister made, write it down and add how it made you feel and what some of your thoughts are about her insensitive remark.

Give journaling a chance, even if it's something that seems outside your comfort or experience level. Don't automatically assume it's not for you. At a conference where I included a short presentation on the value of journaling, one attendee came to me the next morning and said, "To my horror you spoke on journaling yesterday. Last night I went to my room and started writing about how stupid I think journaling is—how I'm sick and tired of hearing people rave about keeping a journal. They go on and on about how helpful it is to them and how it has changed their lives. I wrote that if I hear one more person share the virtues of journaling with me, I'm going to puke."

Kim paused and leaned closer. "I want you to know that when I started to write, I didn't stop until two hours later. After I'd expressed my feelings about journaling, I started writing about how I felt on other issues. I *now* know why I fought journaling so hard for so many years. I realized that when I wrote down my feelings on paper—once they were there in black-and-white—I could no longer deny that was how I felt."

If you identify with Kim's original judgment and the thought of penning and preserving your emotions seems difficult or too painful, start by writing about something small or trivial, such as what you felt and thought when you waited for 15 minutes in the express line of a grocery store because several people in front of you had 20 items instead of the posted 12-item limit. What went through your mind during that seemingly endless time? What would you have liked to tell the cashier, store manager, and the shoppers in front of you?

Journaling also provides a written account of what is happening and the emotional impact in your life. It makes a great reference when you want to remember specific events, and it may be interesting reading for you when a few years have gone by.

Like praying and reading the Bible, journaling helps me express

my feelings, focus on God, and figure out what he wants recycled or
removed from my life. It can do the same for you.

Spiritual Friendships

Spiritual friends provide an opportunity for emotional growth
that is unique and profound. And being involved in a "spiritual
friendship group" is like adding nutrient-rich compost to my summer flowers. The difference these friendships have made in my life
is dramatic and observable.

In his book *Soul Shaping,* Douglas Rumford says,

> A spiritual friendship is an intentional relationship be-
> tween two people, founded in Jesus Christ, in which
> they focus alternately on the nurture of each other's spir-
> itual life. The expectation is not that you be experts, but
> that you come together as spiritual peers who commit
> themselves to growing in Christ.[3]

If you'd like to establish spiritual friendships or a spiritual friendship group, seek the Lord's guidance on who to invite. In my group
there are three of us, which is the right amount to maintain good
communication and emotional honesty. You want spiritual friends
who are willing to be transparent and vulnerable; people who will
not share confidences; and friends who are close to the same level
of spiritual maturity you are. These relationships shouldn't be confused with mentoring, coaching, or counseling. And the time you
spend together isn't for teaching or casually chatting. The funda-
mental purpose is to help each other pay attention to God's hand
in your lives.

Depending on your schedules, you may choose to meet with
your spiritual friend(s) once a week or twice a month. My group
usually starts our time together with prayer, asking Jesus for wisdom
and discernment—that he shows us what he is saying and doing in
our lives. Then each person shares for 15 minutes about their spiritual journey since the last meeting. In preparation for this, I review

what I've written in my journal since the last time we met. People choose to talk about something they saw in a movie, heard in a sermon, and read in Scripture or a book that touched them. Any experience or concern about experiencing God is appropriate.

The listeners' role is to hear carefully and help the person sharing discern what Jesus may be revealing or where he is working. At the end of the 15 minutes, listeners can ask questions that may help identify patterns or themes or share what they discern about how God is working. At one of our recent meetings, my spiritual friends listened to me and asked questions that helped me become aware of the heavy expectations I tend to put on myself and how alone I feel when I'm carrying them.

The purpose of this group is to focus on the work of God in our individual lives. Establish beforehand if questions can be asked of people while they're sharing or at the end of their sharing. As God leads, ask questions for clarification, insights, and encouragement. Questions that focus on Jesus are good. And it's best to minimize the number of questions that call for a simple yes or no response. With Pastor Brian Rice's permission, I've included an adapted list of the helpful questions he uses in his "Soul Shaping" class in case you and your friends would like some help in this area.[4]

- What do you think Jesus was doing in your situation?
- Why do you think Jesus is doing this work at this time in your life?
- What are you hearing Jesus say to you about this issue?
- What were you feeling at the time?
- What are you feeling right now as you talk about it?
- What do you sense Jesus is saying about that feeling?
- How have you prayed about this?
- How have you encountered Jesus when you prayed about it?

- What healthy things have come out of the situation?

- How has this situation been harmful?

- How has this situation been helpful?

- What emotions are you experiencing? (For example, joy, love, peace, hope, comfort, and trust.)

- It seems there is a struggle or tension in this situation for you. Why is that?

- What are the next steps of response you sense Jesus is asking of you?

- How do you feel about taking those steps?

Say Yes and Give God Your Mess

As you practice the strategies we've discussed, such as spiritual friendships, daily times of devotion, praying, reading Scripture, and journaling, set up regular times of self-examination so you stay tuned to what you're feeling. You want to identify and deal with any negative thoughts and feelings God wants you to deal with.

I used to say, "When I get my act together, I will..." I now realize that day will not come while I'm here on earth. Like my garden, I'm in continual process. There are always weeds to pull, bushes to trim, and debris to remove, compost, or toss. My garden is still beautiful even though it's not finished and needs regular maintenance to stay healthy and productive.

We also are lovely to God even though we are still in process and need his continuous help. Never forget that Jesus is our Master at Waste Management. Through modern technology we can take about 20 plastic bottles and turn them into a Polartec fleece garment. But technology fades when compared with the amazing miracles and wonders Jesus can and does do with our garbage. When we give him our irritations, hurts, resentments, guilt, and shame, he uses them to transform us into his likeness and influence others for him in a powerful way. He can make something good—even great!—out of our yuck and junk if we surrender them to him.

Let's say yes to the Lord!

Yes, Lord, I will...

- stop stuffing my emotions.

- discard that desire that has become a demand.

- express my anger constructively.

- let go of bitterness and resentments.

- go through the pain of grief so I can heal and grow.

- face my fears and worries instead of fretting about them.

- expose any lies, guilt, and shame I believe or feel and replace them with truth from your Word.

- set healthy boundaries instead of trying to please people all the time.

- manage my emotional trash on a regular basis.

- trust you to point out areas I need to work on and help me achieve your goals.

Have you cleaned out a drawer or closet and found something of value you forgot you had? I've done that. Often when we clean out our emotional trash, we find a precious part of ourselves we've forgotten or ignored. Once you've composted a difficult loss, perhaps you'll discover a more compassionate part of yourself because you have a fresh experience of what it feels like to suffer. Maybe you'll be less judgmental of people because you realize how hard it is to expose and deal with guilt and shame. Hopefully you'll encourage others more because you've let go of bitterness and experienced the healing power of forgiveness.

Here's a reflection from my journal on the necessity of making the effort to recycle:

> I recycle and am glad I do. I try to be caring of the earth. But at times it is a pain. Now, no matter how busy I am, I must leave the stinky tuna can on my counter until I have time to wash it.
>
> Recycling can be a hassle—a real inconvenience. Wouldn't it be nice if we didn't have garbage? But we do. And I find the type we often forget is our emotional garbage. It is just like other trash. It can stink at times, and it too needs to be recycled, composted, or discarded for the benefit of my world and the world around me.

Eugene Peterson, who created the paraphrased *Message* Bible, describes our sinful nature as "a stinking accumulation of mental and emotional garbage" (Galatians 5:19 MSG). From personal experience I can tell you how much easier that stinking accumulation is to manage when handled as it comes—a little bit at a time.

Instead of stuffing your hurts, resentments, and unrealistic expectations in a drawer or trying to hide your shame and guilt in a dark closet, I encourage you to start recycling, composting, and taking the trash out today. Face your feelings and build healthy relationships so you'll experience more peace and joy every day. Do it for the benefit of your world and the world around you.

TIME TO TAKE OUT THE TRASH

1. Do you tend to be proactive or reactive regarding handling your emotional trash?

2. Which one or two excuses or justifications for ignoring emotional trash do you identify with most strongly? Note a few times when you used them and what the results were for you and the people around you.

3. What time of day works best for you to schedule in a few moments for self-examination? If you haven't set up a specific time, why not do it right now?

4. What changes will you make to allow more time for reflection and trash handling?

"Trash Talk"
Bibliography

Bell, Rob. *Velvet Elvis.* Grand Rapids, MI: Zondervan, 2005.

Colbert, Don, MD. *Deadly Emotions.* Nashville: Thomas Nelson, 2003.

Cornell, Steve. Steve is a senior pastor at Millersville Bible Church, Lancaster, PA.

Eldredge, John, and Stasi Eldredge. *Captivating.* Nashville: Thomas Nelson, 2005.

Goodfriend, Rick. "Anger Management Communication Skills Tip #12," http://ezinearticles. com/?Anger-Management-Communication-Skills-Tip-12—Taking-Out-Emotional-Garbage-Leading-to-Conflict&id=1460800, accessed April 5, 2010.

Hanby-Robie, Sharon, and Deb Strubel. *Beautiful Places, Spiritual Spaces: The Art of Stress-free Interior Design.* Chicago: Northfield Publishing, 2004.

Living Word Community Church, York, PA, Lent booklet.

Mellin, Laurel. "Taking Out Your Emotional Trash," The Soul/Body Connection, http://www.spiri tualityhealth.com/newsh/items/ecourse/item_2841.html, accessed April 7, 2010.

Merges, Hank. "Some People Are Like Garbage Trucks." *York Dispatch* (newspaper, York, PA), Feb. 28, 2010.

Nouwen, Henri J.M. *Life of the Beloved.* New York: Crossroad Publishing Company, 1992.

Olivieri, Penny. Penny is president of Huntington Beach, CA, Aglow International.

Schutt, Randy. "Guidelines for Dealing with Patterned Behavior," http://www.vernalproject.org/ papers/interpersonal/DistraughtGuide.pdf, accessed April 7, 2010.

Smedes, Lewis B. *Forgive and Forget.* New York: Harper Collins, 1984.

Stoddard, William S. *Wisdom from a Pastor's Heart.* Douglas Connelly, ed. San Francisco: Jossey-Bass, 2001.

Thomas, Gary. *Pure Pleasure.* Grand Rapids, MI: Zondervan, 2009.

Truman, Karol K. *Feelings Buried Alive Never Die.* 4th ed. Brigham City, Utah: Brigham Distributing, 1991.

Warren, Rick. *The Purpose-Driven Life.* Grand Rapids, MI: Zondervan, 2002.

Notes

Are You Trash Conscious?

1. The first time I heard this phrase was in a March 2000 sermon given by Robert Wolpert, former pastor for Emmanuel Christian Fellowship, York, PA.

Chapter 1: Are You in the Danger Zone

1. W. Robert Nay, "The Faces of Anger: Short Term Interventions for Change," Wellspan Behavioral Health and Education Series, May 25, 2001.
2. Charles Stanley, *Becoming Emotionally Whole* (Nashville: Thomas Nelson Inc., 2008), 3.
3. Clark Gerhart with Jefferson Scott, *Say Goodbye to Stubborn Sin* (Lake Mary, FL: Siloam, 2005).
4. Cornell University Communications, "Researchers describe how cells take out the trash to prevent disease," adapted, *ScienceDaily*, Nov. 18, 2008, http://www.sciencedaily.com/releases/2008/11/081110154032.htm.

Chapter 2: What Trash Have You Grown Used To?

1. "Water in the Bible: John 7:37-39," http://www.gospel.com/topics/living+water, April 8, 2010.
2. Ruth Haley Barton, *Strengthening the Soul of Your Leadership* (Downers Grove, IL: InterVarsity Press, 2008), 41.
3. John Ortberg, *The Life You've Always Wanted: Spiritual Disciplines for Ordinary People* (Grand Rapids, MI: Zondervan, 1997), 129.

Chapter 3: How Do You Sort Through Your Emotional Trash?

1. "South Central PA's Best Kept Secret: Waste Management Recycle America," *Connections: Working and Living in South Central Pennsylvania*, May 18, 2008, vol. 13, 51.
2. For a more comprehensive list arranged by category, check out http://www.psychpage.com/learning/library/assess/feelings.html, accessed March 26, 2010.
3. John Ortberg, *If You Want to Walk on Water, You've Got to Get Out of the Boat* (Grand Rapids, MI: Zondervan, 2001), 141.
4. Patsy Clairmont, *Under His Wings* (Carmel, NY: Guidepost Edition, 1994), 127.
5. Henri J.M. Nouwen, *The Genesee Diary: Report from a Trappist Monastery* (New York: Doubleday, 1981), 31.
6. Ibid., 74.
7. Oswald Chambers, *My Utmost for His Highest* (Grand Rapids, MI: Discovery House Publishers, 1992), July 30.
8. Dan B. Allender, *Betrayal and the Loss of Faith,* http://www.mhgs.edu/Files/Documents/VFE-1-0/Betrayal-and-the-Loss-of-Faith, 2, April 1, 2010.
9. Daniel Gilbert, *Stumbling on Happiness* (New York: Alfred A Knopf, 2006), 238.

Chapter 5: Are You Recycling Your Anger?

1. John Gottman, quoted in Daniel Goleman, *Emotional Intelligence* (New York: Bantam Books, 1995), 135.
2. Jan Schmalz, "Reader to Reader," *Body + Soul,* March 2009, 20.
3. Sheila Walsh, *Honestly* (Grand Rapids, MI: Zondervan, 1997), 79.

Chapter 6: Who Do You Need to Forgive?

1. Corrie ten Boom and Jamie Buckingham, *Tramp for the Lord* (Fort Washington, PA: Christian Literature Crusade, 1974), 56-57.

2. See www.forgivenessandhealth.com/html/benefits.html, accessed April 1, 2010.

3. Jonas Beiler, *Think No Evil* (New York: Howard Books, 2009), 2.

4. Catherine Marshall, *Something More* (Carmel, NY: Guideposts Assoc. Inc., 1974), 38-42.

5. Tyler Perry, "The End of Fury," *Oprah Magazine*, March 2006, 215.

6. David Stoop, *Forgiving the Unforgivable* (Ann Arbor, MI: Servant Publications, 2001), 26-27.

Chapter 7: Are You Stuck in the Forgiveness Process?

1. David Stoop, *Forgiving the Unforgivable* (Ann Arbor, MI: Servant Publications, 2001), 122.

2. Lewis Smedes, *Forgive & Forget* (New York: HarperCollins Publishers, 1984), x.

3. Oswald Chambers, *My Utmost for His Highest* (Grand Rapids, MI: Discovery House Publishers, 1992), November 20.

4. Clark Gerhart with Jefferson Scott, *Say Goodbye to Stubborn Sin* (Lake Mary, FL: Siloam, 2005), 161.

5. This exercise was inspired by the work of Karen Reivich, PhD, the co-director of the Penn Resiliency Project and a research associate in the Positive Psychology Center at the University of Pennsylvania. She's also an instructor in the Masters of Applied Positive Psychology program.

6. Joy Jacobs and Deborah Strubel, *Single, Whole and Holy: Single Women and Sexuality* (Camp Hill, PA: Horizon Books, 1996), 73-76.

Chapter 8: Which Losses Can Be Composted?

1. Michael Pollan, *Second Nature* (New York: Grove Press, 2003), 81.

2. Therese A. Rando, *How to Go on Living When Someone You Love Dies* (Lexington, MA: Lexington Books, 1988), 15-16.

3. Leslie Vernick, *Defeating Depression* (Eugene, OR: Harvest House, 2009), 39-40.

4. *Recreation Guide to Your National Forest,* January 2009, 1. This came from a flyer I received from a national park. According to the brochure, similar information is available at www.redrockcountry.org and www.fs.fed.us/r3/coconino.

Chapter 9: What Emotional Clutter Is Consuming Your Life?

1. Barry Schwartz, quoted in Marcus Buckingham, *Find Your Strongest Life* (Nashville: Thomas Nelson, 2009), 32.

2. Oswald Chambers, *My Utmost for His Highest* (Grand Rapids, MI: Discovery House Publishers, 1992), Nov. 23.

3. Steve and Sally Breedlove, Ralph & Jennifer Ennis, *The Shame Exchange* (Colorado Springs: NavPress, 2009), 21.

4. Buckingham, *Find Your Strongest Life,* 170.

5. Breedlove and Ennis, *Shame Exchange,* 9-10.

6. Ronald Rolheiser, *Forgotten Among the Lilies* (New York: Doubleday, 2005), x.

7. Ibid.

8. Buckingham, *Find Your Strongest Life*, 246.

Chapter 10: Are You Taking Out Your Trash?

1. Tom Rath and Donald O. Clifton, *How Full Is Your Bucket?* (New York: Gallup Press, 2004), 53.

2. Gary Thomas, *Pure Pleasure* (Grand Rapids, MI: Zondervan, 2009), 126.

3. Douglas J. Rumford, *Soul Shaping* (Carol Stream, IL: Tyndale House, 1996), 381.

4. Questions adapted from Brian Rice, "Soul Shaping" class questions, 2009. Brian is pastor at Living Word Community Church, York, PA. Questions are used by permission. All rights reserved.

ABOUT THE AUTHOR

Georgia Shaffer is a licensed psychologist in Pennsylvania and a certified life coach. She is the author of *How Not to Date a Loser: A Guide to Making Smart Choices* and *A Gift of Mourning Glories: Restoring Your Life After Loss.*

She was featured in the film *Letters to God* and is on the teaching team of the American Association of Christian Counselors' Life Coaching Training series and their DVD series *Conquering Cancer* and *Fresh Start.*

Georgia speaks frequently at conferences, women's retreats, and singles' events. She enjoys helping people identify what needs to grow and what needs to go in their lives.

For additional resources
and helpful information, check out:

www.GeorgiaShaffer.com

To invite Georgia to speak to your group, call:

888-664-5679

HOW NOT TO DATE A LOSER
A Guide to Making Smart Choices

**Are you
…frustrated with dating?
…wondering how to find the right one?**

How Not to Date a Loser helps men and women avoid unhealthy people, build vibrant relationships, and find romance! Christian psychologist and life coach Georgia Shaffer reveals how to…

- pinpoint the qualities you want in a mate
- determine if someone has integrity and is trustworthy
- deepen your capacity to connect romantically
- minimize emotional reactions that can block intimacy
- create a social network that makes life satisfying right now

Whether dating or just starting to date, you'll discover how to steer clear of losers and find emotionally and spiritually healthy people with great relationship potential.

*"Save yourself time and heartache by applying the
principles shared by Georgia Shaffer."*

GARY D. CHAPMAN, PhD, AUTHOR OF
THE FIVE LOVE LANGUAGES AND *LOVE AS A WAY OF LIFE*